EARLY

MARKETING
Playbook

SCALE YOUR ONLINE BUSINESS
TO OUTRAGEOUS SUCCESS

by lisa jacobs

For my five, forever more xx

TABLE OF CONTENTS

INTRODUCTION

I think "marketing" might be one of the least appealing words on the planet. I've always wished I had a better way to describe this subject that I'm obsessed with. I've called it everything from the more personal "putting yourself out there" to the less threatening "talking shop," but nothing seems to do it justice.

As if the word itself wasn't bad enough, the definitions of "marketing" are *terrible*. I love the act of marketing, and I hate every single way it's defined. Except for this sentence, which I found on Wikipedia after a lot of dull and monotonous words …

"Marketing is used to create the customer, to keep the customer, and to satisfy the customer."

The word is terrible and the definitions are even worse, but there it is. Marketing is everything that involves the customer. Its definition should be, "the act or instance of doing business." If a thriving business is what you want to <u>have</u>, then marketing is what you need to <u>do</u>. Simply put, if your business isn't exceeding your expectations, then marketing is the missing link.

Now, here's how it actually applies to you …

You're severely overestimating the reach of your online presence. Your brand is most likely recognized as intermittent and unreliable. You think you're showing up in your potential customers' lives way more than you actually are. You think your outreach is way more significant than it actually is. And all the while, you probably even fear you're overdoing it.

These are the things I aim to remedy once and for all, so let's cut straight to the chase.

In relation to all that's happening on the internet, your business is a tiny speck in an infinite universe. As thousands, then tens of thousands, then hundreds of thousands of people find that speck, your business grows in size, reputation, and credibility.

In *Marketing Playbook: Scale Your Business to Outrageous Success*, I'm going to show you how to create a gravitational pull around your online business that attracts and converts more customers. You'll no longer merely exist online. You're going to learn how to become a force so large with a reach so wide that you'll outshine the competition and corner the market.

Marketing has become a very general term that leaves most business owners feeling overwhelmed. However, "marketing" simply means finding the customers who desire your work, and then pointing them toward it. It's a service you perform for the people who value your talent.

In this book, you'll not only learn everything that marketing your online business entails, but more importantly, I'm going to teach you marketing *that matters to your bottom line*. As a bonus, I'll show you how to increase and expand your presence online. There's an unlimited amount of commercial space available to you, I want you to conquer every square inch of it.

You see, it dawned on me a while back that the majority of online entrepreneurs are running their businesses day-by-day, and all by themselves. If you reflect on that for a moment, you'll realize how disturbing it is. This is the only industry in which small business owners try to operate, let alone succeed in such a short-sighted manner.

I call this frenzied approach to business "the daily scramble." Most online entrepreneurs wake up today and ask, "What am I going to do *today* to get more sales already?" And then the scramble begins …

"Why, I'll send an email! I'll promote this post on Facebook! I'll make four new items and list them in my storefront, and then I'll tweet and Instagram each of them so everyone will come check them out."

Sound familiar? I can promise you a serious businessperson doesn't scramble, she schedules. A real businesswoman doesn't try something one day, check stats, and give up! No, she persists. She continues to pursue her goals.

Online business is truly the land of unlimited profit potential ... *if* you're willing to do the work. You can't look at the face of an online entrepreneur's successful business and forget all that goes into the operation behind the scenes. I liken it to the workings of a car; the beautiful body you see sitting on the wheels is not what makes the machine run.

Showcasing your expertise with strategic marketing is the antithesis to the daily scramble, so if you're ready to cure panic and chaos once and for all, you're in the right place.

Sales for the Win

During my 10-year career, I've built and succeeded at two different types of businesses. I'll refer to both of these in examples throughout this text. The first was a product-based online store, the Energy Shop. I marketed the shop to sold-out success, and during its run, it was in the top 2% of highest earning storefronts on Etsy.

The second is my service-based business and blog, *Marketing Creativity*. I offer marketing strategy in the form of books, online courses, and private consultations. My revenue exceeds a quarter of a million dollars annually, putting me in the top 8% of highest earning websites on the internet.

I know how to make businesses make money, and nothing matters online unless customers stick to it. My marketing strategies have a laser-focus on the numbers that matter in business, and not views, visitors, and followers.

This is something I discuss regularly with the majority of my blog readers who love to watch stats! They say,

"Yes! My views are up!"
"Oh no, my views are down!"
"I'm not getting any views! What's going on?!"

If you asked these stat-lovers, views are the new currency … only, they're worth nothing. If I have 1,000 views on my storefront and $0 in sales, those are terrible results. If 1,000 people visit my blog, *Marketing Creativity* and 0 people subscribe to the email list, that's an EPIC fail.

Views without sales mean my storefront's not doing its job, which is to sell my product. Views without subscribers mean my blog's not doing its job, which is to connect me with like-minded entrepreneurs on the build.

A typical online business strategy looks like this …

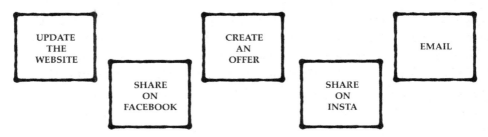

These are random acts of marketing that are not meant to stand alone, as most people use them. They're tactics being spontaneously misfired, rather than a strategy being deployed. I'm going to show you how to combine your efforts inside of a profit-winning strategy. Your customers will finally be able to rely on you, and in turn, you will finally be able to rely on your business.

Before We Begin

While easy to understand and implement, the strategies within *Marketing Playbook* are advanced. The material assumes you have a few things in place …

1. An online point of sale such as a storefront, website, blog, etc.— somewhere where potential customers can actually check-out and buy from you
2. A product for sale (this could be a service, information, or an actual product that needs to be shipped, but it assumes you have something to sell)
3. *Some* interested buyers (you've proven the marketability of your product; you know people are willing to pay money for it)
4. An email list manager

If you have these four items under your belt, you already have more resources than you realize. You've got all of the components of a working sales machine, now it's simply time to build it! If you're in the researching stages of your business and one or more of these aren't in place yet, I've included instructions on how to achieve them in the **appendix** of this book.

My strategies are user-friendly and easy to comprehend. That's intentional. One of my strongest (and most satisfying) suits in business is breaking down complex theory into its basic concepts, and showing others how to apply that information for effective results.

At the end of this book, I've included a list of marketing terms in the **glossary** (e.g., mass marketing, permission-based marketing, direct response marketing, unique selling proposition, and much more!) where you'll find the definitions and a summarizing thought on each. I wanted this text to be as comprehensive as possible, but more importantly, I want you to walk away with simple strategies that produce meaningful results right now.

Just as tactics shouldn't be confused for strategies, the terms in the glossary are for basic intel. In and of themselves, they shouldn't be confused with the formulas that will help you grow and profit online.

Finally, you should be able to build and execute the formulas learned here within a month's time. This isn't an overdrawn, theoretical lesson; quite the opposite. It's an effective organization of the resources you already have available to you.

Thirty days is plenty of time to create the systems I laid out for you in this playbook in a calm, methodical manner. Where prompted, assign deadlines to your systems and follow through on them <u>no matter what</u>.

Chapter 1

MARKETING THAT MATTERS

If you've been in business online for any time at all, I bet you've seen your share of marketing headlines, such as ...

- 21 Ways to Spread the Word about Your Business
- 10 Surefire Ways to Get Found Online
- 18 Ways to Market Your Online Business
- 101 Resources for Marketing Your Business

These are absolute time wasters, guaranteed to fuel your daily scramble and make your marketing efforts less effective than before you read the list of "helpful" advice.

If you go down any of these lists you'll find tips such as, "Share your work on Facebook." We're all doing that anyway. But what makes these generic lists even more dangerous is that it's marketing for marketing's sake. There's no plan behind it, there's no strategy, and there's certainly no cure for the scramble to be seen. Anyone could do those lists of things and millions already are. It's white noise.

There are three foundational rules to marketing that matters.

#1 A Consistent Message

Because it exists online, your business is sending a perpetual message to the world whether you set it up intentionally or not. As you sit here reading this book, that message is being spread for you.

That's the beauty of online business, but it can also be the curse of it. What is your business saying for you if your updates appear …

- unfinished,
- rushed,
- neglected,
- non-existent,
- desperate,
- stale,
- mismatched, or
- sporadic?

Quite a bit, I imagine. What you put into your business, it puts out to the world. Nobody wants a stale offer that's been ignored by others and is now gathering dust on the virtual shelves of your business' storeroom.

As humans, your customers are susceptible to a perceptual phenomenon called "change blindness." It means we cannot see that which does not move. I liken it to driving along a highway when you suddenly catch movement of a deer in your peripheral vision. You were essentially blind to the sidelines before that deer moved.

When we apply that concept to your customer, it is safe to assume that if you're not moving toward them, they're not thinking about your business at all.

Therefore, constant and consistent movement is paramount to your success. The underlying movement between buyer and seller is the best part of business. It's a dance, and it can be perfectly choreographed to create maximum enjoyment for all.

But if you're not already dancing, they can't join in. You're always the lead partner.

That's why you want to send a consistent message. It should always be seeding future growth in the relationship between you and the customer. The heart of your communication should be the answers to these two questions:

1. What specifically are you promising the customer?
2. How does your offer serve them?

For example, I offer my clients strategic planning and rapid growth in online business. My website offers free advice and informational articles on those topics. My Instagram demonstrates actual planning and growth strategies from my journal. My Pinterest account is geared toward a well-designed life and business. My Facebook conversations revolve around profit- and growth-related topics.

#2 A Customer-Centric Focus

Marketing is not about what you want from the customer. That's a me-centric approach and part of the frantic scramble for sales. And why are online entrepreneurs scrambling? Easy! Because …

- I want more sales!
- I need more traffic!
- I want your email address!
- I want a reliable income for myself, and I want this business to provide it!

If you listen closely, that's what makes up the white noise of all the daily scrambling taking place online. It starts with, "I want your …" and it ends with "money in my pocket." Anyone can say that. We're all saying that!

Instead, customer-centric marketing is about the solution you have to offer, and how it will meet the customer's needs.

To stand out on a crowded internet, shift your headspace to a place of giving. In business, as in life, you wouldn't want to get to know anyone who made everything all about themselves. Figure out how to nurture a natural give-and-take friendship between you and your customers, and you'll be a best-seller for sure.

In the opening, I mentioned that you're a tiny speck in a vast and ever-expanding space, as we all are in internet business. But when we zoom in closer, let's imagine your speck has the unlimited potential to grow and fill all the empty space around it.

Your marketing system is all of your outreach efforts in orbit. With this book, you will create an eccentric force (a push that creates a rotational movement) by creating a consistent message that attracts the right customers. The more customers you attract and retain (orbiting your business), the more powerful its gravitational pull.

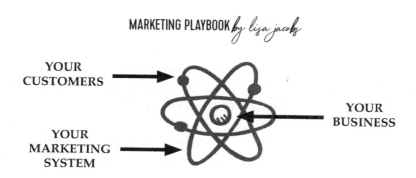

The most exciting thing about an effective marketing system is that it makes the right customers want to *populate* your business. Your customers will never belong to your business, but they will feel as though your business belongs to them.

Your customer doesn't care about you or what you want, and your marketing will not take off until you fully understand their motives. Instead, the customer is always asking, "What's in it for me?"

Listen to this advice from *Scientific Advertising* written by Claude Hopkins in the 1920's:

"Remember the people you address are selfish, as we all are. They care nothing about your interests or your profit. They seek service for themselves. Ignoring this fact is a common mistake and a costly mistake in advertising. Ads say in effect, 'Buy my brand. Give me the trade you give to others. Let me have the money.' That is not a popular appeal."

Think about your own shopping habits. Do you make purchases with the business owner in mind? Of course not! But you do buy from businesses you feel "get you" in style, presentation, and offer.

You must get to know your customers just the same, if not better. To do so, you'll need to create an in-depth ideal customer profile [CHAPTER 2]. It starts off as guesswork and a general idea, sure, but it evolves over time into glorious business relationships.

There is as much to know about your ideal customer as there is your spouse or best friend. Before I met my spouse, he started off as a general idea too. I'm attracted to men, so I knew he would be male. I wanted to have lots of children, so I knew I'd need a man of good character that I found very attractive. Oh, and most important of all, he had to make me laugh!

I've now been married for twenty years and counting. We have four delightful children together. The relationship I have with the man I married has evolved into the most valued partnership of my life, but he too started out as guesswork.

In other words, you won't know everything there is to know about your ideal customer right now, but start to get to know them anyway. They're important.

#3 A Long-Term Strategy

Every year, I release an annual productivity workbook and online business planner titled *Your Best Year*. It's about 150 pages dedicated to helping online entrepreneurs plan for and commit to their biggest dreams. And every year, without fail, countless individuals write to let me know how the book saved their business, because what it actually does is save the owner's commitment to their business.

The hardest thing about online business is weathering the slow seasons. There will be times when it feels as though you're talking and no one's listening, you're selling and no one's buying, or you're reaching but no one's connecting. Keep doing it anyway.

In this book, I'm going to help you build and launch your own marketing strategy. Once you get started, it's important NOT to give up no matter *how you feel* about your business, because how you feel is not an accurate measuring stick for success.

Your commitment is the only thing that can guarantee your strategy wins.

Together, we're going to create an online machine that will attract new visitors, engage them, and convert them into actual paying customers—automated to run in your absence. That said, you're still the wizard behind the curtain.

The Buying Process

Before we dive into marketing, let's understand how the customer comes to find your business online. First, let's look at the buying process in the physical world. When you leave your house to go shopping for a specific item in an actual store, you …

1. enter the store,
2. scan the aisles for what you want,
3. spot the item you're looking for,
4. pick it up and handle it, and
5. decide to buy.

Now, we'll look at the buying process for online shopping, which is somewhat similar. When you shop online, you …

1. search for the product you want,
2. scan the website,
3. click on the item that interests you,
4. read about it, and
5. decide to buy.

Regardless of where you're checking out—store, website, or online storefront—what's important to notice is the underlying movement of the buying process. There's a pull, a driving force, a strong desire toward the product, and then later, the decision to buy.

It's time to make this process the best experience imaginable for your ideal customer.

Chapter 2

THE MARKETING SYSTEM

To kick off the marketing system and everything that falls underneath that umbrella of activity, I want to give you the big picture behind these concepts. At the heart of your efforts is always this formula:

⚙️ ATTRACT > CONNECT > CONVERT

Through the strategies in this book, your marketing will be designed to reach potential customers, connect with them in an authentic way, capture their attention, and ultimately convert them to paying customers.

This umbrella includes the basic ingredients of a winning marketing campaign. It can be overwhelming to see all the things listed individually, but when they're combined your marketing system becomes an effective and automated solution for your business.

1. IDENTIFYING   **THE MARKETING**
2. REACHING   **UMBRELLA**
3. ENGAGING
4. ESTABLISHING TRUST
5. CONVERTING
6. FOLLOWING UP

This is your marketing system. It's made up of six tasks that all fall under the general term "marketing." In other words, marketing means always doing these six things:

1. Identifying who your potential customers are
2. Reaching your potential customers
3. Engaging with your potential customers
4. Establishing trust with your potential customers
5. Converting potential customers into actual customers
6. Following up and building relationships with actual customers

I've always explained online business as a web of connectedness. My social media accounts and advertisements at the outermost level (reaching new potential clients for my business) with the center of my web being the point of sale.

As my business has grown over the years, this has taken on a three-dimensional vision, and I no longer see online performance as a flat-laid web, but rather a planetary sphere with its own orbit.

As you grow in business, your presence—the amount of people you attract, connect with, and convert—grows as well. Growing larger (aka scaling) becomes easier, because you're no longer a speck in the midst of vast and limitless space. Instead, you become a massive presence commanding attention in the industry.

Whatever you share online lives there, like a growing orbit of attraction. The more space you claim, the more space becomes available to you. The more movement you generate around you, the more momentum you gain as a whole.

This Is You

That is the ultimate goal of your system—to be growing your orbit. To do so, it must be performing the following six tasks all of the time.

#1 Identifying an Ideal Customer

If you say, "My product is for everybody," you might as well say it's for nobody. It's very important that you narrow your target market so that you can better understand how to appeal to your niche audience.

The big question is: Who is the perfect customer for my product?

Her style, personal taste, and budget will perfectly match your brand. Imagine the ultimate fan of your work by writing up a description of just one person on paper. There are a million things to explore about your ideal customer, but let's start here:

- Is she married or single?
- What age range does she fall into? (e.g., 18–24, 25–32, 33–40, etc.)
- Does she have children?
- Does she spend a lot of time on the internet?
- Which websites does she frequent?
- Which magazines does she subscribe to?

Depending on the product you're selling, some of these questions won't matter much for your ideal customer, but others will hold vital information. There are a lot of clues about where you can find your potential customers online and how you can approach them hidden in the answers to questions like these.

For example, if your ideal customer doesn't spend a lot of time online, she probably only frequents major websites, such as Facebook and Pinterest. Therefore, you'll learn that you're wasting your time trying to find potential customers on industry blogs … where she's probably not hanging out. You can then focus your marketing efforts where you know you can find her.

#2 Reaching Your Potential Customers

This step is critical to your growth, and the most often overlooked! As online entrepreneurs, we make a product or perfect a skill, build a business around that product or skill, and then forget that it's also our job to find all the customers the business needs.

There are several ways to reach your potential customers, and I list them here from most effective to least effective:

- Direct Contact: Email and newsletters
- Referrals: Peer and customer word-of-mouth recommendations
- Live Audience: Featured speaking, teaching, or webinars
- Blog and Social Media: Writing and communication
- Industry Shows and Events: Local displays and appearances
- Paid Advertising: Pay-per-click, sidebar/banner, and print ads

From a quick glance of the list, you can see that email marketing is king while other time-consuming tasks, such as building a booth at a local show, are often highly overrated.

The big question is: How do people typically find products like mine?

Appearing before a live audience is near the top of the list because it adds instant credibility when you're called to speak or are otherwise showcased as an expert in your industry, and it can take years to reach the well-known status it requires.

Direct contact via email, on the other hand, is something you can (and should) implement into your business plan immediately. Make sure the things you do and the places you spend your time online help you reach your potential customers.

#3 Engaging with Your Potential Customers

Creatives often get themselves caught under a "jack-of-all-trades" category. Because we operate like that, the branding is often askew and mismatched, the message is all over the place, and while it's a subtle layer of psychology that most entrepreneurs don't pay attention to, your potential customers become confused.

A successful business needs to be one face, one brand, and one source of expertise for their customers. It needs to have a clear purpose in order to stick.

Therefore, you want to hone in on what it is you have to offer your ideal customer. Always start with the customer's need. Whether you fill a void in their life by offering information or inspiration, make their house feel more special by creating home decor they love and adore, or make them feel more complete and confident by giving them that one special accessory for their outfit, whatever it is, there's a purpose for your product in the customer's life, and it's your job to clearly identify and communicate it.

The big question is: What's in it for them?

Matter of fact, don't think of it as a product or a purpose. Think of it as a solution. There's emotion attached to solutions. As business owners, we need to breathe in that emotion—fully absorb it and own that expertise—and then share it with everyone we touch.

#4 Establishing Trust with Your Potential Customers

The recipe for a trusting customer is made up of proven authority, credibility, social proof, and reputation. It's something that is built over time, but there are parts of your expertise that you can showcase to speed up the process.

The big question is: What makes me the best person for the job?

Wherever possible (on your landing pages, website, and social media accounts), be sure to share your brand's social proof. From Wikipedia,

> "**Social proof** is a psychological phenomenon where people assume the actions of others in an attempt to reflect correct behavior for a given situation. This effect is prominent in ambiguous social situations where people are unable to determine the appropriate mode of behavior, and is driven by the assumption that surrounding people possess more knowledge about the situation."

In other words, the best way to get new people to see your work is by having a lot of people already looking at it. It's a conundrum, for sure, but my motto is: *hack it until you have it*. We'll work around this obstacle throughout the book.

Social proof helps the customer feel "at home" while shopping with you. On Etsy, it's the combination of history and experience (as well as the site-familiarity that Etsy provides) that helps the customer trust the transaction.

Social proof can also come from word-of-mouth, product reviews, and brand recognition (i.e. "Oh! I've heard of the Energy Shop before! My best friend LOVES her bracelet.").

You can help your customer find your business' social proof by using phrases such as, "best-selling," "back by popular demand," and "previously sold out" on items that have a history of doing just that. Your customers are influenced by people with similar tastes, and they're automatically attracted to that which they perceive as popular.

#5 Converting Potential Customers into Actual Customers

Too often, people feel entitled to sales simply because they listed a product or service online. There's so much more to it!

The big question is: What makes my customer want to buy?

Sometimes you release your glorious, passionate creation into the world and nobody even notices it's there! How many times has this happened to you? And how many times have you ditched the new offer altogether out of sheer disappointment?

Disappointment is a real danger in passion-based businesses. It will cause you to drop a project when it doesn't get off the ground as you'd expect.

That's why, for every new project I release, I launch it with a 3- to 6-month marketing plan. It is not enough to create a product, you also have to make sure people know about it. Oftentimes, the first announcement is only the beginning of the campaign.

#6 Following Up and Building Relationships

Many online entrepreneurs see a sale as a one-off deal, but to me, it's the beginning of a beautiful relationship that I will treasure for years to come.

The big question is: How can I WOW them?

You are the expert in your field. The customer came to you because you have knowledge and/or talent that they appreciate. That means your point of sale is full of items that they want. Own your expertise, and be the enthusiastic salesperson your business needs.

1. IDENTIFYING   **THE MARKETING**
2. REACHING   **UMBRELLA**
3. ENGAGING
4. ESTABLISHING TRUST
5. CONVERTING
6. FOLLOWING UP

These six tasks fall under the umbrella of what your marketing is meant to do for you. It's your marketing system's job to cover all of the above tasks, and you employ your blog, online storefront, email list, and social media accounts (the touch points of your sales funnel) to get the job done. You want to intentionally design each space you create online so that it performs at least one of the six required tasks at all times.

For example, once I <u>identified</u> who my ideal customers are, I use my Instagram and Pinterest accounts to <u>reach them</u>, and my blog is written to <u>engage and establish trust</u> with new visitors. *Marketing Creativity* does that effectively by answering many problems my ideal customers face, while simultaneously showing my experience and knowledge of the industry.

My email list is also good for establishing trust, as I have an automated responder sequence that goes out to new subscribers to better introduce my business to people who have just found me online.

When I meet a potential customer, let's say you've just found my article on Pinterest, I am not asking for the sale. That honestly wouldn't be good for either of us [in the service industry. However, it's perfectly fine to ask for the sale on the first encounter in retail]. I am, however, subtly asking whether or not my teaching style is a good fit for your business. Am I providing valuable information for you?

I continue to establish trust with my potential customers through various articles, newsletter updates, and free offers. It's via email that most potential customers will <u>convert</u> into actual customers.

Chapter 3

THE CUSTOMER
FLOW CHART

In order for your marketing system to be doing all six tasks, you need to create what's known as a "sales funnel" which I like to demonstrate with my customer flow chart. It's made up of all the landing sites and touch points in which visitors will find you.

I use this customer flow chart (aka "the sales funnel") in training all the time. In itself, the image is pretty basic. However, it's important to note that this is not actually a funnel with an end puddle. Instead, it's a cycle.

New customers are invited into the funnel, and then encouraged to come back around. It's designed to continuously build better relationships and more referral business.

I like to layer bigger business lessons onto this image, as I'm going to do here.

At the top of the sales funnel (where you see referrals, blogs, shops, and social media accounts pouring in), you'll find the widest opening. Up there, you're talking to a lot of different people at once: you're introducing yourself to new visitors and engaging long-time fans and customers with the same breath.

At the opening, you're having friendly and casual conversations, but when combined with the strategies of your marketing campaign, it becomes purposeful and effective.

Your online storefront, blog, any referrals, and all of your social media accounts feed into the top of the customer flow chart.

When those visitors start to listen and engage with the content or products you're sharing, they move closer to your sales funnel. They're interested, or maybe even just curious about what you're saying. They lean in; they want to know more.

This means that you're not just gaining one-off traffic, but you're actually speaking to your ideal customer's challenges and interests.

At this stage, something about your business appeals to the potential customer, and they think you could be a solution in their lives. This is where the average online business owner's marketing efforts stop. But as you can see, it's still a very superficial relationship; we're just getting started.

The best way to connect with the potential customer and move the relationship forward is to collect emails during these early stages. Have sign-up forms, opt-ins, and offers regularly running on your social media accounts and website in order to encourage visitors onto your list. This is called opt-in conversion [CHAPTER 5] and you should aim to convert at least 10% of all website traffic and social media followers into email subscribers.

Next, you start to establish trust. Beyond social media and public posts, you begin to answer their questions. Your emails provide insight, value, and add another layer of intimacy to the relationship.

Your potential customer may not have said "yes" to the sale, but they're definitely listening and feeling a sense of connection.

Like any other relationship in life, this one takes time. The rhythm of your emails, the consistency of your message, and the value you provide builds rapport.

At this point of the customer flow chart, your potential customer is a resounding "maybe."

They're getting to know you. They're growing to trust you. They believe you might be the person for the job, and when you have sales conversations, they're listening.

THE "YES" LINE

In order to convert more sales, you have to ask for more sales. And trust me, there doesn't have to be anything salesy about it! In this book, there's a whole section dedicated to the beautiful art of selling [CHAPTER 9], but right now I need to talk to you about your customer's answer to that ask.

Typically in online business, you create a product, list it online, and then see the customer's next action as a very black-and-white move. They buy or they don't. They will or they won't. They're always either a YES or a NO.

But that's not how you shop! Impulse buys and door-to-door sales pitches are a thing of the past because of … the internet. You have all day to compare prices, choose your best options, and read reviews. If

THE "YES" LINE (CONT'D)

you're still unsure about the purchase, you can jump on Facebook and ask your friends what they buy to receive instantaneous feedback.

When you make an offer via email, this is how you perceive your customers will receive it …

those who answered YES	*those who answered* NO
👥👥👥👥 👥	👥 👥👥👥 👥
👥 👥	👥👥👥👥 👥

After you make the offer, you figure, if they said yes—great, they have the product now; if they said no—oh well, maybe next time.

This is where your customers actually stand when you make an offer, projected onto your sphere of business.

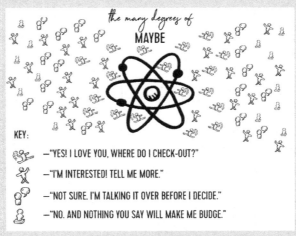

the many degrees of
MAYBE

KEY:

—"YES! I LOVE YOU, WHERE DO I CHECK-OUT?"

—"I'M INTERESTED! TELL ME MORE."

—"NOT SURE. I'M TALKING IT OVER BEFORE I DECIDE."

—"NO. AND NOTHING YOU SAY WILL MAKE ME BUDGE."

All of the people between not interested and YES! are strong maybes. When you don't follow up on your offer or follow through with your marketing campaign, you leave their business on the table.

The majority of people in and around your customer flow charts are strong maybes. They're out there right now, and they're anticipating your next offer.

You convert your first sale. This funnel had a broad, wide-open start, but now we're talking about a single transaction. A new customer has entered the customer pool, and you now feel a sense of knowing one another. You're engaged in an active exchange of energy.

At this stage, you've effectively moved your customer from a place of "maybe" to a place of "yes!"

Finally, the follow-up. Because you never want to treat a new customer as a one-off sale. The after-sale is your opportunity to build a relationship, and all good businesses are built on good relationships.

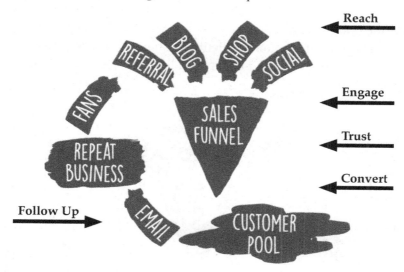

Regardless of where your customers are checking out—store, website, or online storefront—remember the underlying movement of the buying process. There's a pull, a driving force, a strong desire to the product, and then later, the decision to buy.

CUSTOMER FLOW CHART EXAMPLE

Let's bring the marketing system to life by using my client, Megan of yourcoachmeg.com, and her marketing system as an example.

MEET YOUR COACH MEG

Megan is a certified life coach whose motto is: *Life's a party … let's plan it!* Both her website branding and online persona are so alive, it's difficult *not* to be drawn to her.

She offers her clients free consultations, one-on-one life coaching, group coaching, and a VIP package. In this exercise, she'll be selling her one-on-one coaching program, *Your Life, Perfectly Balanced.*

In the following example, the customer flow chart represents the online presence Megan has built for her business. The product is at the bottom because the potential client can't have it until she buys, and the ideal client, who's not even sure she wants a life coach, is placed at the top of the flow chart.

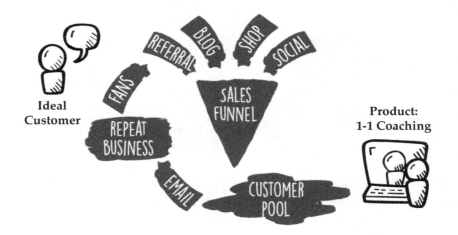

 This is Lindsay. She's an ideal customer profile I built for Megan's business. Lindsay is surrounded by good friends and family, and she loves them dearly, but she's never felt lonelier. She's about to turn 34, and she recently broke off a dead-end relationship. She feels stuck in a job she doesn't love. Seemingly overnight, she went from passionately charging toward her dreams to sleepwalking through her existence. She craves a spiritual awakening, and she's looking for guidance.

Lindsay first saw Megan on Instagram, but she very well could have found her on Pinterest or Facebook. Lindsay was drawn to Megan's colorful photographs and inspirational quotes immediately. She felt brighter just looking at Megan's style.

Lindsay followed Megan on Instagram. She understood immediately that Megan was a coach who was full of inspiration (it helps that her handle is @ yourcoachmeg), but Lindsay didn't identify coaching as something that would benefit her.

This is very common customer behavior. When a potential client shows interest on social media, it doesn't mean they're interested in what you do (or make) *yet*. If you *pushed* them to buy at this point, they'd run for the hills.

Megan continued to use her business Instagram feed to share small, but powerful inspirational tips. The advice is easy to digest, and it gets her followers on their feet, ready to take action. Lindsay finds herself looking forward to every update.

Megan posts a client testimonial that says, "Thanks to Coach Meg I am now living the exact life I was dreaming about." This hits Lindsay like a ton of bricks because she's not only missing out on that life, she's *stopped dreaming* about anything at all. She's stuck in a rut, and she finally realizes how deep it runs.

People tend to make-do with what's not working in their lives way longer than is necessary. The example of Lindsay's realization is a pivotal point in her and Megan's relationship, but it may have taken months for her to come to it. It still may be months before Lindsay takes the next action (to buy).

This is where email encouragement is <u>a must</u>. Opt-in offers should be sprinkled into the feed (about every 6-9 posts), giving followers a reason to subscribe. The next action (buying a coaching package) is going to be an intimate exchange of value. While Instagram is more intimate than most platforms, it is still a social media (to be seen, not necessarily acted upon).

Lindsay feels a little worried for herself. How did she get here? How did so many of her dreams slip through her fingertips? When did she lose herself? She ponders questions like these for a few days. She's had an awakening of sorts, but her life still feels rather lifeless. She's not sure what to do about it.

 Just because you awaken a desire within a client or customer does not mean they automatically see you as a solution. They will learn to know their desire *first*, and it's your job to keep appearing in their life as the solution or source.

Lindsay is still following Megan on Instagram, but her desire for more LIFE! in her life is growing, and she's tuned out on social media. It's all a distraction from her newfound self-discovery, and she wants to create real change in her life now more than ever.

Thankfully *for them both*, Megan's got her email. She posted an opt-in offer, *Seven Small Acts to Great Change* that Lindsay signed up for weeks ago.

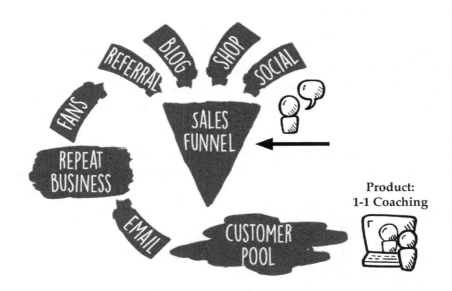

Product:
1-1 Coaching

If this seems like a lot of work for one client, remember the orbit. Lindsay is not the only potential business Megan's attracting. She simply represents all potential customers at all the many stages of "maybe."

Because of regular email contact, Megan has the best chance of being the solution to Lindsay's problem as her desire to change grows.

Throughout this time, Megan shares blog posts and sends email updates that leave Lindsay feeling uplifted and inspired. Megan writes, "seek progress, not perfection." She tells Lindsay through an especially touching email to "be patient with yourself as you evolve." Lindsay starts to notice that she feels calmer the day Megan's emails arrive. She thinks back and remembers all of those Instagram updates Megan shared that made her feel better, too!

For the very first time, Lindsay thinks "Maybe I need a life coach."

All the while, Megan's been sending a message about her services. Her copywriting is basically a loving hand on your shoulder. In essence it says, *it doesn't have to be so hard. There's an easier way. Let me help; I've got your back.*

Product:
1-1 Coaching

At this point in the process, Megan has reached the potential client, engaged with her, piqued her interest, awoken her desire, and gained her trust. The next steps are to convert and follow through with excellent service.

Unbeknownst to Lindsay, Megan approached her semi-annual promotion to recruit new clients (she knows there are a lot of "maybes" looming around her orbit, she strategized this promotion to invite them in).

She updates her social media profiles to tell everyone who's "ready for dramatic results" to be on her list for an exclusive coaching offer. She writes a series of five emails in one week. They are informative and thought-provoking, and she sells her coaching package at discount in each one. Lindsay signs up on the fourth email.

Still, Lindsay is nervous! This is the first time she's ever spoken to anyone off the internet. Within seconds, Megan's branded new client package lands in Lindsay's inbox. It explains the entire process, shows Lindsay what each call will be like, and tells her how to prepare.

Lindsay smiles and takes a deep breath. She made the right decision.

Chapter 4

MARKETING GOAL

Now that we've covered the marketing system and sales funnel, it's time to create a marketing goal. You'll name one for every strategy you build and promotion you run.

Every good marketing campaign should have a desired end result, and that end result should substantially contribute to your business' bottom line. You should be able to measure the success of your campaign in metrics of both growth and profit.

A marketing goal is much different than big picture business goals you might set, such as "I want to make $80,000 this year" or "I want to double my annual salary." Your marketing goal is essentially a mile marker towards these ambitions.

It's a smaller goal with a shorter deadline that feeds into the bigger picture. It represents what you hope your marketing efforts will achieve, and it helps you determine what to focus on throughout the campaign.

Without setting and sticking to a marketing goal, you'll wind up in the daily scramble.

It's all too easy to get caught up in doing for doing's sake in online business. You might make products even though your current inventory's not moving (making for making's sake), post status updates online even though what you're saying isn't connecting (marketing for marketing's sake), email because you know you're supposed to (emailing for emailing's sake), and research everything you can find online to try to make what isn't working work already (training for training's sake).

You probably find yourself getting swept away by a lot of business-building ideas that don't even make sense: such as, "Open another storefront" (when you already have one storefront that's not selling), or "Grow my account on Twitter" (when none of your customers/clients even use that platform), or "Start Periscoping" (because it's the latest random advice floating around *all of the other* social platforms that day).

None of it matters. It's all doing for doing's sake. You don't need two storefronts anymore than I need two blogs! It will only create more things that don't matter to fuss over. It's scrambling, and you're better than that! Your work deserves more attention, your time is extremely valuable, and your business is meant to give back!

To grow a successful online business you need (1) a website that attracts and converts, (2) a marketing strategy that wins, and (3) a plan to optimize numbers one and two.

Therefore, don't open more storefronts if the original site isn't working. Instead, spend your time and energy improving your existing storefront! Don't start new social media accounts if you're not connecting with the profiles you already have. Instead, study the platform with the most potential to grow your following through the roof!

In online business, you've likely heard of the Pareto principle (aka the 80/20 rule) which states that (from Wikipedia), "For many events, roughly 80% of the effects come from 20% of the causes." For example—and those of you who have an email list will know this to be true, 80% of your revenue comes from 20% of your customers.

The reason this rule is examined in the online world is because it's a hack for doing more of what matters to your bottom line. If 20% of your working hours produce 80% of your results, then that means that the other 80% of the time you spend produces only 20% of your desired results. How would your results improve if you focused all of your attention on the 20% of work that adds to 80% of your bottom line? That's what we're here to explore.

Answer the following questions to find out which 20% of your applied efforts are producing 80% of your desired results:

 WHAT WAS YOUR BIGGEST BUSINESS PAYDAY OF ALL TIME?

 WHERE DO YOU INVEST TIME & ENERGY WITHOUT RETURN?

MARKETING PLAYBOOK *by lisa jacoby*

Your working hours should always result in one of two things:

1. Growth (Will it attract email subscribers and traffic?)
2. Profit (Will it make money for my business?)

If it doesn't result in either of those things (meaning, you're fussing, checking, or otherwise doing for doing's sake), it's not helping your business' bottom line. When you write a list of tasks you need to do for your business, always ask: To what end?

*   To what end are you building another website?
*   To what end are you blogging?
*   To what end are you making more listings?
*   To what end are you tweaking your branding?
*   To what end are you creating a new social media account?
*   To what end are you emailing?

I encourage you to keep your big picture goals front and center (i.e., "Earn $80,000 this year") with the understanding that each marketing goal you set should feed into it.

For example, my business goal for the year is to welcome 1,000 new members to my private training program, the Luminaries Club. A good marketing goal for this <u>month</u> is to create a campaign that supports that ambition.

Therefore, before you post another blog or share another picture on Instagram, ask yourself …

*   What has to happen this year in order for me to feel like an absolute success?
*   How much business (sales/customers/etc.) do I have now?
*   How much business do I need to have by the end of the year?
*   What can I do next month to work towards that?

You may have just created a marketing goal, but hold on a second!

Question your goal to make sure there's not a better way of doing things. For example, many of my clients wish for "more wholesale orders," but I'd hate to see you off on a marketing campaign with the intention of finding more work at your own expense.

"You don't want to get to the top of the ladder only to find out you had it leaning against the wrong wall." —Jack Canfield

I've done my share of wholesale orders through the Energy Shop. Trust me, direct sales double the profit and cost half the work. When people look for more wholesale, I try to read between the lines. What they really want to feel is fulfilled and busy. What they don't yet realize about wholesale is that they'll more likely feel underpaid and resentful. Right ladder, wrong wall.

Another way to make a good marketing goal even better is to question whether or not you can repurpose the promotion or campaign. A rich business is always built on long-term assets.

Before I create a new product, I strategize asset potential. I'll ask myself questions, such as: How can I extend the sales life of this product? When can I repurpose this campaign? What's the offer's shelf life? Is it possible to create long-term, passive income from this product?

This line of thinking has caused me to drastically change the face of several of my offers and dramatically increase my profits over time.

If you have a product-based business, you might struggle with creating assets in which you are not physically or materially involved. You can build promotional, design, and marketing assets instead (while you'll still be involved, it will save you massive amounts of time in the long-run).

For example, you can repeat your designs (do the photo styling and copywriting once with endless relistings), and you can run the same successful email promotions bi-annually, or even seasonally.

Over the years, I've learned that nothing is more profitable than a repeatable marketing campaign. Because you learn so much from every promotion you run, they only get better (and you get more confident about them) over time.

How to Set a Marketing Goal

Let's start with what's NOT a marketing goal, and that is social media fans or followers. It's a vanity metric. Now don't get me wrong, I love Instagram. It's a social media hangout full of interaction and engagement. If left unchecked, I could take and share pictures all day!

I have a great following on there, and personally, it leaves me feeling supported and connected. That said, it's strictly a hobby. I only think about the content for my account in my spare time because, while Instagram doesn't hurt my business, it doesn't help it much either.

Sales (the money that makes the business go 'round) are a very intimate thing, especially in service-based businesses like mine. The customer invests their trust and loyalty in exchange for caring and quality. The sales conversation that encourages that intimate exchange of value cannot take place in the caption of an Instagram post.

Social media platforms do not qualify as a point of sale. They're at the very top tier of the sales funnel; therefore, in the grand scheme of things, a place to have very superficial conversations. Yet I know online entrepreneurs spend the majority of their marketing efforts here! That means that you are spending 80% of your marketing efforts on platforms that are producing way less than 20% of your results.

Social media fans and followers are created *in the wake* of a strong marketing campaign, they're not the goal for it. Why? Because the end result of attracting more Facebook fans are more Facebook fans. That in no way contributes to your growth or profit because most sales conversations will be conducted via email.

Your marketing goal should be based on activities that make money. What's the number one activity that makes your business money?

For example, my number one income-generator is content (in the form of courses, books, and training). Private consultations are a close second. When I'm doing either of these, I generate substantial hourly wages.

When I build a marketing strategy, it's focused on the specific content I want to sell. A marketing goal is always …

- number of sales,
- dollar amount to earn, or
- number of interest-based email subscribers to gain.[1]

These goals will immediately result in growth and/or profit for your business, and that's what you need to market. Your entire strategy should revolve around profit-generating solutions for your business versus …

---

[1] This is less common and ideal for a very high-priced service. For example, if I were offering expensive private consultations, I would seek qualified clients and publicly promote free training seminars (in exchange for email addresses) several months in advance of my available openings.

- growing your Instagram account,
- getting more engagement on Facebook,
- getting more views on a product that's not selling, or
- getting more readers to your blog.

The above are tactics, and yes, you can perfect your tactics (to fine-tune your overall business machine), but do not confuse them for successful end results or marketing wins.

In business, it's sales for the win!

Chapter 5

IDENTIFY YOUR BASELINE

It's time to identify your baseline (starting point). This is going to be essential for, not only measuring your results over time, but also boosting your morale throughout this crazy adventure!

 HOW MUCH DID YOU EARN (AFTER EXPENSES) LAST YEAR?

 HOW MANY EMAIL SUBSCRIBERS ARE ON YOUR LIST?

 WHAT'S YOUR WEBSITE'S AVERAGE NUMBER OF MONTHLY VISITORS?

Now that you have the numbers, you're going to evaluate exactly how your business is performing by calculating conversion rates. When you strive to improve conversion performance, your marketing goals work double-time.

Let's calculate your **sales conversion rate**. In other words, for each promotional email you send, we're looking for the percentage of email subscribers that actually buy. Open your email list manager and pull up the last sales email or campaign you sent. Then, plug the numbers into this formula:

# of sales ÷ # of email subscribers (at time of send) = ☐ x 100 = ☐ %

For example, let's say I sent a sales announcement and discount coupon to 8,000 subscribers. It resulted in 140 sales. The equation would look like:

140 sales ÷ 8,000 subscribers = .0175 x 100 = 1.75% sales conversion. (A good starting rate is .05%, average industry conversion is between 2-3%. Anything above that is high.)

There's yet another metric that's equally important to your business' bottom line, and that's your **opt-in conversion rate**.

In other words, for every visitor that lands on your website, we're looking for the percentage of people that subscribe to your email list. You'll need to open your website statistics and your email manger for this exercise. Plug last month's numbers into the following formula:

#opt-ins last month ÷ # of visitors last month = ☐ x 100 = ☐ %

For example, let's say I had 3,000 visitors to my website last month, and 250 people signed up for email updates.

250 opt-ins ÷ 3,000 website visitors = 0.0833 x 100 = 8.33% opt-in conversion. (A good starting rate is 2%, average industry conversion is 5%. Anything above that is high.)

With your baseline established, it's time to challenge yourself. In the coming year:

 HOW MANY EMAIL SUBSCRIBERS WILL YOU AIM FOR?

Good starting point: 1,000

 WHAT SALES CONVERSION RATE WOULD YOU LIKE TO ACHIEVE?

Good starting point: 0.5%

 HOW MANY VISITORS PER MONTH WILL YOU AIM FOR?

Good starting point: 2,000

 WHAT OPT-IN CONVERSION RATE WOULD YOU LIKE TO ACHIEVE?

Good starting point: 2%

Chapter 6

MARKETING MINDSET

In marketing an online business, there are only two methods for getting more customers to your website, and they're quite simple: you find them or they find you.

The truth about online business is that it's all a numbers game. Once you have a successful platform built, you can scale it however you'd like. If you make 1 sale, that's a clear sign you can easily make 100 sales. If you make 100 sales, you can confidently project 1,000 in the near future!

But if you're not making sales or you're unsure how to scale your business, you first need to know how to reliably and consistently find new customers, and then you need a system in place that helps new customers continue to find you.

Striving Versus Thriving

Now, when you think about all of the businesses online—the good, the bad, and the ugly—notice that they each fall into one of two categories:

Type 1: People that constantly struggle to get traffic, make sales, and profit online. If they do find a customer, it's almost always the worst situation imaginable. The customer wants to barter, trade, get a discount, request a custom order (and never come back to actually pay for it), get a refund, and oh yeah, their package got lost in the mail.

— *or* —

Type 2: People whose products or services are flying off the virtual shelves. These people seem to have a raving crowd of fans at the ready and eager to buy. They mention a product on Instagram, and within minutes, it's sold out! Customers are raving and showing off their purchases (thereby creating even more insatiable desire for the product).

Next, let's imagine how both of these business owners feel about their clients/customers, and let's be really honest with this exercise. I'm going to have you play the role for both parts.

Type 1: The Business that Constantly Struggles

You put your product online for sale, but you don't trust your customer will find it, understand it, or be able to afford it. You've tried marketing, but nobody's listening, so what's the use?

You add more options and customizations, just in case it will add that "something special" your visitor hasn't been able to find anywhere else.

If a customer inquires about a purchase, or actually makes one, you talk a lot. You send a lot of messages and extra confirmations. You're secretly afraid they'll change their mind or they won't like the purchase. You don't want a negative review, and you definitely can't afford to send a refund. Your business needs every sale it can get!

(By the way, I have a successful business, and I can relate to almost every line I wrote above. I've felt all of it, at one time or another over the years. I don't know an online entrepreneur who hasn't experienced the same fears and doubts.)

Type 2: The Business that Constantly Thrives

You put your product online for sale, and you just know it's going to be a huge hit. You set a (too big to admit out loud) sales goal and exceed that insanely glorious figure! When you share or post online, your message is received with warmth and excitement.

You trust your instincts, and that allows you to keep your operation simple. Customers are raving, referrals are pouring in, and people are proud to do business with you!

You know your ideal customer so well that it has allowed you to create a system that surprises and delights them time and time again. You tested the system; you can trust it to eliminate customer confusion and unnecessary conversations.

What Makes the Difference?

Sales always involve two parties: the seller and the buyer. That's you and who's ever on the other end of your sale, preferably your ideal customer.

That makes every angle of the sale dual-sided, and I love to shed light on both. You'll have hesitations about making the ask. They'll have hesitations about making the purchase. You're waiting for them to show interest and find you online. They're waiting for something, *anything* to interest them online. You're afraid they won't buy. They're unsure about buying from you.

As we get into sales and strategies, we'll need to explore both sides starting right here.

Treat Them Like They're Rich

Sue Bryce is a photographer that teaches a mix of photography and business for CreativeLive. *I love her.* In a recent class, she discussed the attitude we bring to sales, value, and pricing.

To paraphrase her beautiful talk, she told a story about what it's like to walk into a boutique where the sales clerk looks at you like you can't afford the product versus what it's like to walk into a boutique where the sales clerk treats you like you're a very important person, or as my children say, "VIP—Very Important Peanuts."

Think about how differently those two situations make you feel. One boutique scenario leaves you feeling utterly dejected, while the other leaves you feeling absolutely rich.

Next, let's look back on our two types of business owners. This is so important: Which person trusts their customer? The one that sells, of course!

Which person is unknowingly rejecting their customer? The one that struggles, obviously. Therefore, never secretly worry that your customer can't afford your product! Don't do that!

Treat them like they're rich. People are drawn to and want to purchase from business owners that trust them. Your customers are important and their time is valuable. Respect them as such to attract more of them to your business.

That's how you fix *their* side of the equation. Next, let's talk about you.

Starving Artist Versus Hungry Entrepreneur

Lately, I've been fixated on the mindset gap between a starving artist and a hungry entrepreneur. Let's compare.

The starving artist mentality is one of sacrifice and suffering. They're more likely starved mentally and spiritually rather than physically, unable to feed an insatiable craving for validation. They exist in a state of helpless desperation, too rejection-weary to persist. Starving artists convince themselves that success means selling out, but this is simply a justification used to excuse their lack of business-building efforts.

— *or* —

The hungry entrepreneur mentality is one of opportunity and determination. This is a person on the hunt for their next win. Starved for nothing, they seek a personal vision of success and take complete responsibility for its realization. Hungry entrepreneurs are on the build, primed for their next chance to create the results they desire.

See the difference?

Now, let me give you the choice. Which personality above do you want to buy from? The hungry entrepreneur, of course! You aren't going to shop a weary excuse of an offer. You're not attracted to needy desperation. You don't want to give your money with an added tip of reassurance and validation. Nobody *chooses* to be drained by emotional vampires!

More importantly, which personality are you going to choose to be?

The starving artist mentality is the path of least resistance. It's easy to make excuses and justifications for why you're not achieving your desired results. Anyone can want and not change. Anyone can name their weakness and excuse it as incompetence. Most people do!

If you're going to be a hungry entrepreneur, you have to be responsible for your results 100% of the time. Tony Robbins says, "If you want to take the island, you have to burn the boats." Start showcasing your strengths and stop babying your weaknesses. When you avoid your pain points it only serves to prolong them.

I don't care who you are, human beings are attracted to leaders and winners. They're drawn to true performers who are willing to take the stage.

In order for people to receive your business with warmth and excitement, you must believe in its success and your abilities long before you ask for a sale.

What Makes the Customer Buy?

I'm an experienced copywriter, and I love to teach the methodology behind the words and techniques that bring sales. You probably know the textbook definition of copywriting, which is to write in a persuasive way that markets, advertises, and raises brand awareness. And yes, it's all true, *but it's so much more than that.*

Copywriting is an advanced sales technique that adds movement and brings life to your online business. It's the language that builds relationships online, and I teach an eight-week training program designed to help you learn and perfect that language. It helps you sell in the most authentic way imaginable, leaving both you and the customer feeling triumphant in the end.

I could write a book about this technique, and maybe I will. But for now, I need to give you a few tricks of the trade to ensure that the marketing strategies you set up in this section will win.

Let's talk about what specifically your online content (social media shares, blog posts, email newsletters) should be saying in order to get your customer to a place of "Yes! I want to buy that." In fact, I call these the "Six Triggers to Yes" in my online training programs.

Remember the many degrees of "maybe"? People engaged with your brand are at varying stages of "yes," "no," and "maybe" at all times.

Let's imagine each of those potential customers has an internal buying thermometer, and that everything you say online either warms them up (gets them closer to the sale) or cools them off (pushes them farther from the sale).

Obviously, you want everything you say online to warm your customers toward the sale. Therefore, you're going to want to employ the following six triggers in your social media updates, promotional blog posts, and routine email newsletters. They'll expedite the time it takes to get your potential customers from "maybe someday" to "yes right now!"

Here are the six triggers to "YES!"

THE SIX TRIGGERS

1. CONVERSATION
2. AUTHORITY
3. RECIPROCATION
4. SOCIAL PROOF
5. ANTICIPATION
6. SCARCITY

Incorporating these six triggers may take more thought than you're used to when writing online. Copywriting doesn't come naturally to most. However, the lovely thing about the written word is that you do the work once and then it lives forever, continuously greeting customers past, present, and future.

#1 Conversation

To engage with potential customers is to master the art of online conversation. Before posting online, ask yourself: How would I warm up to this conversation in real life? Anytime I'm writing something challenging online, or when I can't figure out where to start, I imagine the person I need to talk to is standing in front of me.

If I'm about to create a sales campaign for my services, I imagine my neighbor—whom I barely know—has a need for my offer. Would I walk up to her home, knock on the door as I was taping pictures of myself onto her windows and pushing brochures through her mail slot, and then stick my card in her face when she came to answer the door? Of course not. That would be utterly obnoxious. Yet, that's how the majority of people approach their customers online.

Instead, I would treat her like the person she is and start a conversation addressing her issues and how my services could solve them. It can and should be relaxed, casual, and comfortable for all parties involved.

Back on our customer flow chart, the conversation is taking place at the top of the funnel. If you'll recall, there your marketing's responsibility is to reach

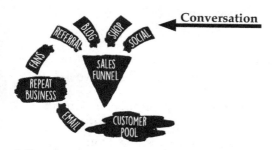

Conversation

and engage. Keep the conversation casual yet inviting to leave your customer with a sense of comfort and belonging.

Just like with any new introduction, early conversations should be light, casual, and held on common ground. Consider the following prompts, and how you might work them into social media status updates and blog posts:

- Find common interests—what is your ideal customer thinking about today?
- Brainstorm ways you might help each other—"I'm looking for a new photo editing app. What's your favorite?"
- Think of ways you can prompt them to share hobbies/interests—"I'm trying a new recipe today. What are you baking for the holidays?"
- Show off your familiarity with the industry—share pictures of you with industry friends, the aisles of supply shops, your work in progress, etc.

#2 Authority

Oftentimes, online entrepreneurs (and every other career-oriented person, for that matter) attempt to claim a position of authority by rattling off degrees earned, universities attended, jobs had, awards given, accomplishments achieved, etc.

To a potential customer just meeting you, none of what you think makes you an authority matters. They're on the other side of that speech asking, "What's in it for me?" And you're leaving them with nothing to take away.

Another mistake creatives make is using big fancy words for techniques and supplies. For example, I just finished a bullet journal spread in my Leuchtturm1917 with a Muji 0.38-mm tip. True story.

But unless you're an expert at the same hobby, that sentence would only serve to frustrate you. Therefore, what I said to impress my knowledge and authority upon you actually backfires in a big way. If I'm the expert and you're the novice, the best way I can impress you is by describing what I'm doing at your level of understanding.

This: I just finished a bullet journal spread in my Leuchtturm1917 with a Muji 0.38-mm tip.

Becomes this: I drew a monthly calendar in my notebook using my favorite gel pen. It's how I track and record my progress each week.

The best way to show your authority to potential customers is to meet them at the level of experience they possess, speak in a language they understand, and relate to the problems they're trying to solve. Don't *try* to impress them; simply leave a good impression.

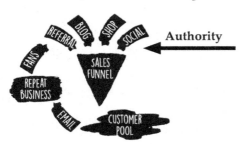
Authority

Authority is still high at the top of the customer flow chart, but it's not questioned by repeat customers. Quite often on my blog posts, and in order to establish my authority for newcomers, I'll make statements such as,

"My strategies are always geared toward helping you make more sales."

Those one-liners are inserted for the people just finding me after clicking an image on Pinterest. I don't need to email that, or tell my clients I can help them make sales—they already know this about me. My authority's been proven and established.

One of my favorite suggestions for proving authority is to share a behind-the-scenes look at one of your techniques. Especially if you fear nobody's buying your product because they think they can make or do that themselves.

Use a round of social updates to tell people one of your trade secrets, and show them some behind-the-scenes footage. Customers love those extra layers of product information, and if they had any doubt before, they'll soon learn they can't DIY that job. They want to buy from the best, so be the one that provides that authority in the marketplace.

#3 Reciprocation

Reciprocation is the idea that whatever you invest into the relationship between you and your potential customer is paid back in kind.

The essence of the reciprocity trigger is that your instinct to reciprocate a favor will overpower your inclination to say "no." It's the most frequently exploited of the six triggers, and for those of us who don't like the idea of cold-selling what has been made with a warm heart, this tactic can feel like a back-handed nicety.

However, I love this trigger because it reminds us to constantly aim to earn more traffic and sales by first giving, then asking. There must be a constant exchange of value.

We exchange our product for cash. We exchange an enticing offer for an email address. We exchange the time we spend on social media and branding for customer loyalty and followers. We exchange time invested in new creations for steady website traffic. We exchange promotions for an increase in sales and revenue.

In the spirit of fair exchange, don't wait for the sale before you consider what you'll offer the customer for their time and consideration.

In service-based businesses, information is generally packaged and given away in exchange for an email address. In product-based business, a future discount is typically promised in exchange for an email address.

Reciprocation falls further down in the sales funnel. It's part of the trust-building stage, and it happens when the potential customer becomes engaged.

#4 Social Proof

This one is tricky to achieve, yet extremely necessary to possess. Social proof means that we're automatically attracted to what we perceive as popular, and skeptical of everything else.

As discussed in the marketing system, the best way to get new people to see your work is by having a lot of people already looking at it. It's a conundrum, for sure. This trigger leaves many new online entrepreneurs stuck at the bottom of the totem pole.

Every online business needs social proof because it's a powerful influencer. During the buying process it provides reassuring evidence. Strong reviews and testimonials will get potential buyers over the hump of indecision. It also builds trust and credibility for your brand.

Once gained, social proof will provide tremendous momentum for your business. For example, it took enormous amounts of time and energy to gain 250 email subscribers in my first year of blogging. Years later and with plenty of social proof to back me, I gained 2,500 new email subscribers *last month* without effort.

The good news is, if you need social proof you can hack it until you have it. Do so by joining Pinterest group boards in your industry, find Facebook groups for promotion, or sign up for a private membership program, such as The Luminaries Club. These are all designed to help you boost your marketing efforts online.

Whatever social proof you do have, you want to flaunt it. Post reviews received, repost customer images shared, and always look for new ways to encourage more feedback and engagement.

As for our customer flow chart, social proof belongs everywhere, all the time. It will appeal to past, present, and future customers alike.

#5 Anticipation

Building a sense of anticipation around a new product or promotion is vital to its success.

Too often online entrepreneurs ask for the sale in a very one and done manner. Sellers put something new out, and if it gets customers—great. If it doesn't, they see it as rejection. Failing to build anticipation and lack of follow-through leaves many sales ("maybes") on the table.

There are dozens of ways to build anticipation for an upcoming offer, to include:

- Share sneak peeks of the project in the making
- Have someone photograph you photographing the new product
- Host a pre-order special exclusively for your email list

- Post early-bird access on your favorite social media platform
- Tell everyone on social media to "Subscribe to my list for the biggest sale of the year!"

As any good marketer will tell you, the promotion dates are actually the middle of the campaign. Here's how I usually run my launches:

- 3 months before: Announce product and release date
- 6 weeks before: Regular mentions and reminders of release date
- 7-day launch period: Everything's about the product, all the time
- For 3 months after: Regular mentions and reminders that the product exists

This lesson will come to life as we get into marketing strategies [CHAPTER 7] because, as you can see, anticipation falls much further down the sales funnel in our customer flow chart.

It's also a great technique to add to the other triggers we've covered. A little anticipation spices up conversations (upcoming sales are fun to hear about), sometimes invokes reciprocation (especially when you're treating your email list like they're part of an exclusive inner circle), and builds social proof!

Regardless of what's actually going on with sales, when you're sharing and building anticipation for an upcoming promotion, people will assume that because you're graciously keeping the public informed "everyone" must be interested. It's another way to hack social proof until you have it.

#6 Scarcity

Before we discuss scarcity, I need to show you what shopping online looks like for your customer. First, think about how long you *think about* some purchases. Have you ever …

- Browsed an Etsy shop for weeks, and though you love and adore the product, you still haven't made the decision to buy?

- Daydreamed of an expensive addition for your home, but talk yourself out of making the investment over and over again?
- Added a much-needed book to your wish list, then left it sit there for months?

Why do we do this? It's simply human inertia. From Wikipedia,

"**Inertia** is the resistance of any physical object to any change in its state of motion, including changes to its speed and direction. It is the tendency of objects to keep moving in a straight line at constant velocity."

Whenever you create a new product or run a seasonal promotion, you need to create a sense of scarcity to help the buyer overcome that resistance to the purchase. If your product is available forever, the potential customer might think about it for just as long (or forget about it altogether)!

On the customer flow chart, scarcity is closer to the sale. It's a technique used to get people over the "maybe" hump so that they become a member of your valued customer pool.

There are three standard ways to use this trigger effectively: (1) limited number, (2) limited time, and/or (3) special pricing.

For example in a product-based business promotion, I emailed my list:

"As a thank you for being part of my mailing list, here's an exclusive preview to tomorrow's big sale! Many items in stock are limited edition, and as always, you get first dibs. Come see what's new and enjoy 30% off your entire order!"

It's a limited number (the product will sell out), a limited time (one night to shop before tomorrow's public sale), and special pricing (30% off). Even though the sale will publicly run for three days, and as you'll soon see in the next chapter, this email will generate 80% of the profits.

Chapter 7

MARKETING STRATEGY

Your marketing campaigns will be designed around the upcoming calendar year and your business' strongest seasons. This strategy enables you to keep your priorities in order of importance: Your life *then* your business. It will not only help you eliminate the daily scramble, it also guarantees you'll improve your results and enhance your career.

First, look at the coming year and identify where you'll need time off, such as summer vacation, winter holidays, important dates, back to school, etc. List these special events on your calendar before listing business-related projects or promotions.

In the example exercise below, I've noted all of my personal time with a star ⋆.

JANUARY	FEBRUARY	MARCH	APRIL
	⋆ *weekend break*		

MAY	JUNE	JULY	AUGUST
	⋆ *summer break*	⋆ *vacation*	⋆ *back to school*

SEPTEMBER	OCTOBER	NOVEMBER	DECEMBER
	⋆ *weekend break*		⋆ *downtime*

I'm still working where you see personal notations, but it's important to bring awareness to the events to ensure I leave plenty of space for them.

For example, I tend to go stir-crazy in February, and it messes with my emotions and my outlook. I made a note to plan a long weekend away that month. I like to spend a lot of time with my children during summer break, so I made note of when school's out and back in session. I love to take December at a slower pace so that I can shop at leisure and bake for days without worrying about my schedule.

Notice that these personal occasions are on the calendar long before any product or promotional launches, and you can see my year already starting to take shape. I'm obviously not going to launch a new course or host a busy promotion in December (or worse, as a last-minute scramble for business) because I've already claimed white space in my calendar that month. I can set up the rest of the year to ensure I get time off.

I'm always looking for ways to improve my work-life flow. When I notice something I love or dislike about my schedule, I take note. Some examples are:

- I dislike projects that drag on for longer than three months
- I'm desperately craving a retreat/getaway this time of year
- I'd like to purely focus on the family during this holiday or occasion
- Take a personal day once a month

Strive to constantly gain more intel on your routine and schedule. The creative energy you spend in this business is an expensive fuel to burn. If you don't continually replenish that energy, you'll quickly gas out and fail to meet your goals.

The next thing you're going to add to your calendar is your busier seasons. If you have an existing business, you can check your annual statistics for the months where you get most traffic. If not, you can use my examples as a guide.

It is the nature of business to have hot and cold seasons, most do. This technique is in place to help you utilize those seasons to their fullest. For example, it seems like everyone is on the internet in January, whereas in February, nobody's online. There will be plenty of average months in between, but it's important to take note of the high and low tides in particular. I've noted seasons with a bullet •.

JANUARY	FEBRUARY	MARCH	APRIL
• everybody>internet	★ weekend break		• nobody>internet
	• nobody>internet		

MAY	JUNE	JULY	AUGUST
	★ summer break	★ vacation	★ back to school

SEPTEMBER	OCTOBER	NOVEMBER	DECEMBER
	★ weekend break	• everybody>internet	★ downtime

 With full awareness of your personal schedule, as well as busy and slow seasons, it's time to plug in the **money makers**. There are many different ways your business can earn money, but I'm going to advise you to specifically name three to six money makers.

These will be the larger promotions or projects that anchor your entire year. When scheduling your money makers, be sure to avoid the slow seasons and steer clear of your personal occasions. Here's my example of a service-based business (with my blog as the point of sale). Money makers are noted with an arrow →.

JANUARY	FEBRUARY	MARCH	APRIL
• everybody>internet	★ weekend break	→ Playbook	• nobody>internet
→ copywriting course	• nobody>internet		

MAY	JUNE	JULY	AUGUST
→ Shop 2.0 course	★ summer break	★ vacation	★ back to school
		→ coaching	

SEPTEMBER	OCTOBER	NOVEMBER	DECEMBER
	★ weekend break	• everybody>internet	★ downtime
	→ Your Best Year		

Here is an example of a product-based business (with a storefront as the point of sale).

JANUARY	FEBRUARY	MARCH	APRIL
• everybody>internet	★ weekend break	→ bi-annual sale	• nobody>internet
→ New Year special	• nobody>internet		

MAY	JUNE	JULY	AUGUST
→ summer launch	★ summer break	★ vacation	★ back to school

SEPTEMBER	OCTOBER	NOVEMBER	DECEMBER
→ bi-annual sale	★ weekend break	• everybody>internet	★ downtime
			→ free shipping

So much is revealed when big projects are added to the annual calendar. Rather than be stifled by slow seasons, you can use them to your advantage and work ahead. You can prepare, promote, and create excitement around the next big event. You can make your best-selling seasons even better.

With this big picture in mind, you will know when your efforts will be rewarded.

Your annual strategy will also help you determine when to stock up on inventory, when to work ahead, when to take a break, and so on and so forth. *Marketing Playbook* is designed to help you strategize and build marketing campaigns, this calendar shows you when to deploy them.

Your business rises and falls according to the effort you invest. When you know your seasons, you can create your own peaks and crests rather than become victim to them.

Use the form on the next page to plug in your personal time, seasonal tides, and money makers. Then, we'll talk about what you need to do to make it happen.

MARKETING PLAYBOOK *by lisa jacobs*

YOUR ANNUAL STRATEGY

MONTH OF:

Your Best Year Plan

In my best-selling productivity workbook, *Your Best Year*, I created a plan that earned me a huge profit breakthrough in business. Each year, I do four specific things that help me exceed goals and shatter income ceilings. I make my …

- goals resolute,
- strategies specific,
- system efficient, and
- action plan productive.

In this section, I'm going to show you how to do the same. First, let's cover some fundamental principles of goal-setting.

Your New Business Manager

Your goal should be your business manager. In other words, you should always be reporting to it. Gauge your success by whether or not you're meeting its expectations. Your goal is counting on you to get the job done.

As we've discussed, your goal should always result in growth or profit, and preferably both. One usually feeds the other. Growth brings more profit, and more profit brings faster growth.

Your goal for the next twelve months should be a game-changer; something that's guaranteed to take you to the next level of your career. It should test your boundaries and stretch your comfort zone. Some examples are:

- Build my email list to 12,000 subscribers, tripling its current size (growth).
- Earn $102,000 this year, doubling my previous year's salary (profit).

In my early days, I spent entire years focused on growth. I looked at the start-up of my online business as though I were building a portfolio for my clients. I spent the majority of my days blogging, mentoring for free, and creating a library of opt-ins.

Now that I have a substantial foundation in business, I shift my focus between growth and profit. I prefer to set income goals because it's an umbrella to all strategies, as you'll see in the upcoming examples.

Next we'll cover marketing strategies and action plans, but keep in mind that you will always work backward from the year's main goal. Remember the daily scramble? A typical online business strategy looks like this …

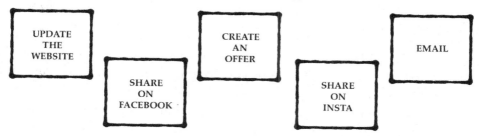

With the *Your Best Year* Plan, you'll never wonder what you should be working on again. Here's a look at the complete system.

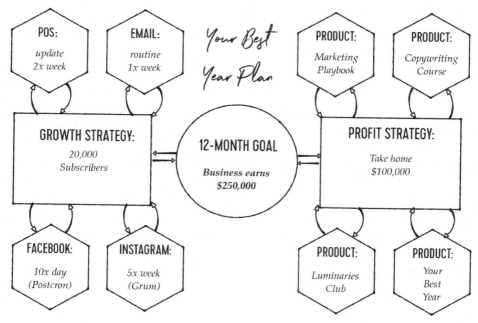

See the difference?

In the first graphic, tactics are being misfired as strategies, each one only answering its own purpose (doing for doing's sake). The activities aren't connected to each other, and they won't result in significant progress.

In the second graphic, every activity has a purpose. Every money maker has a target. Notice how smaller activities always funnel into a larger strategy, they're systemized where possible, and each one ultimately feeds the goal.

To compare these two approaches in business to physically reaching a destination, it would be like …

1. leaving your house with no destination in mind, making a series of random left and right turns as you go, and aimlessly driving in circles until you run out of gas versus …
2. leaving your house with a destination in mind, a timeline for getting there, and a GPS to guide you.

When working on your business, always ask: Does this activity feed my goal?

For example, my annual goal is to welcome 1,000 new members to my membership program, The Luminaries Club. This would enable me to hire club counselors, create an ongoing support system, and have more time to make valuable educational tools and resources.

Therefore, I question everything on my to-do list. Will it help me reach that goal?

Will checking Facebook or Twitter 23 time a day help me welcome 1,000 new members? Absolutely not. That's why I'm rarely there anymore. Will Pinterest help me welcome 1,000 new members? A little bit. I give it about 20 minutes per day. Will writing an epic blog post that gets pinned 1,000 times help me to achieve my goal? You know it. That's the work I need to focus on!

Anytime you start fussing over your schedule or looming to-do list, I want you to question what you're doing, and more importantly, WHY you're doing it.

The Strategies

Once you have a goal in place (and it's both resolute and firm), it's time to develop the strategies that will help you achieve it. The strategies are divided into our two main categories: growth and profit.

Your growth strategy consists of all the places you build and market your business online: your point of sale (POS), your email list, and two to three social media platforms where you reach and connect with your ideal customers. The systems you use are what automates as much of these activities as possible, such as Postcron (a social media scheduler) or Grum (an Instagram scheduler).

Your profit strategy consists of the money makers (three to six annual products or promotions) you named at the beginning of this chapter.

Let's look at my example graphic again, paying attention to where these take effect …

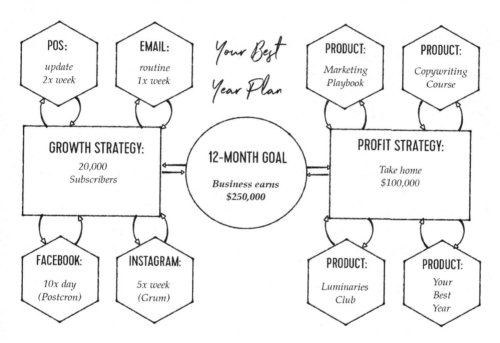

The Action Plan

We want your action plan to be as productive as possible, so before I send you off to create your own *Your Best Year* Plan, let's assess your current operation.

Keeping your goal for the next twelve months front and center, ask yourself what activities you're willing to commit to all year in order to achieve it. Your challenge is going to be to continuously move the needle toward progress even when you're not getting immediate results. Remember, each small step gets you closer to the destination.

The real secret to success is persistence. You must keep trudging along even when it feels like nobody's buying, listening, reading, caring, supporting, or sharing. Are you willing to go the next year at full speed toward your desired results?

Your Growth Strategy

Your POS is the website or storefront where you offer your product, and the hub of your online business. Your POS could be the blog where you offer digital products, your Etsy storefront where you offer a handmade product, or the website that houses similar content. At what frequency will you commit to refresh that site with new products, blog posts, or information?

 HOW OFTEN ARE YOU GOING TO UPDATE YOUR POS?

Next, consider what would be an appropriate level of email newsletters and updates. There's no "one size fits all" to any of these questions, especially this one. I email my blog readers an average of once per week, but I only emailed my product-based business an average eight times per year. It doesn't matter the frequency you choose, but do commit to a routine.

 HOW OFTEN WILL YOU EMAIL YOUR LIST?

What social media platforms do you not only reach out, but also connect and engage with followers? Most successful online business owners dominate one or two social media platforms (not all). I advise my clients to avoid being everywhere, connecting with no one. Instead, pick your two most successful platforms (three max), and focus on enhancing your presence there.

 WHICH SOCIAL MEDIA PLATFORMS WILL YOU USE REGULARLY?

HOW OFTEN WILL YOU POST ON EACH PLATFORM?

Finally, how can you make your operation more efficient? Look for systems that will automate your workflow so you don't have to touch or "check it" daily.

 ### WHICH TASKS CAN BE BATCHED, SCHEDULED, OR OUTSOURCED?

Your growth strategy will require time, training, practice, patience, and small investments in scheduling software, but it will all pay off exponentially.

Your Profit Strategy

Next, look at your profit strategy. This consists of products or promotions (your three to six money makers) for the year. You want to list each money maker, how much you'll charge (or average sale amount, if it's a product promotion), and then write a target for how much money could potentially be earned.

This will help you project whether or not the money makers will add up to the desired income goal, after taxes and expenses are deducted.

I like to spread my major promotions out, leaving eight to twelve weeks between the next big sale. Here again, there's no "one size fits all." You know the seasons of your business better than anyone.

Your profit strategy requires traffic (online visitors), planning, training, copywriting, marketing, and later, an investment in advertising. This plan ensures that each activity feeds the goal and keeps your operation running like a well-oiled machine.

It's time to build *Your Best Year* Plan.

Your Best

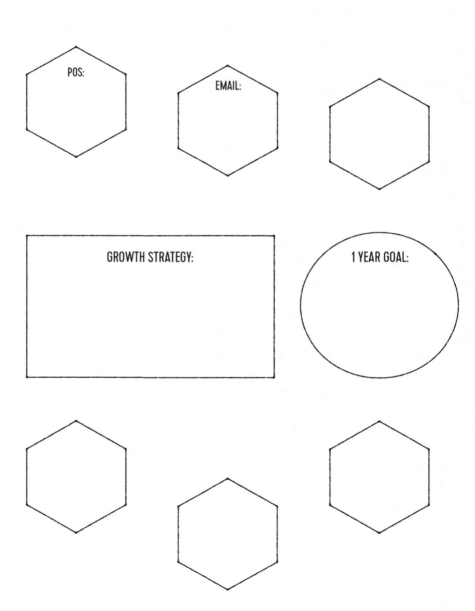

POS:

EMAIL:

GROWTH STRATEGY:

1 YEAR GOAL:

Year Plan

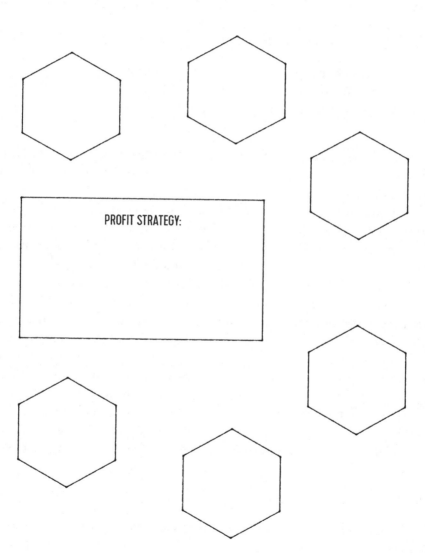

PROFIT STRATEGY:

MARKETING PLAYBOOK *by lisa jacobs*

Dominate the Territory

Success is an ongoing investment in yourself. It's never one and done, although I often wish it was! If you conquer the plan you just built, trust that you will be called to conquer bigger and better goals the next time around.

Marketing is a constant presentation, and the ultimate goal is to dominate space and claim a stake in your industry.

In Grant Cardone's *The 10X Rule*, he states:

> "If you march into any battle without the proper troops, supplies, ammunition, and staying power, you will return home defeated. It's as simple as that. It's not enough to occupy a territory. You have to be able to keep it."

When I read that, I immediately thought of the board game, Risk. If you've never played, it's a strategy game—a battle between players to dominate global territories.

Each player has an army that has to be spread out across the playing field, and whenever you take a new territory, your armies are severely depleted. If you're not fully prepared to, not only go into battle, but also occupy and defend the territory once you take it, you'll quickly lose it again.

From a marketing standpoint, that quote makes so much sense. Have you ever shared something, then felt it fizzle out within moments? It's as if you called the attention of a roomful of people expecting their audience, only to watch them glance up and then go right back to what they were doing.

When you create a marketing campaign, you want to be everywhere, all the time. Encompass your potential clients with your offer. Who are your troops? What supplies do you need? How much ammunition will it take to hold down the territory? Are you doing enough to be remembered?

When I sit down to create a marketing campaign for a new product launch, this is where I start. **As an example**, this is what my early strategy looks like each year when launching *Your Best Year* in October.

What's the product and who's it for?

Your Best Year is a productivity workbook and online business planner. It's the only workbook on the market that's specifically designed for creative entrepreneurs.

70

Who are the troops?

The Luminaries Club members and pre-order customers. Luminaries get a free paperback copy in exchange for an honest review. Subscribers of my email list get an exclusive 40% off coupon code for their pre-orders. This gets the book into thousands of hands before its actual launch date.

What supplies do you need?

I need 1,500 copies of the paperback, envelopes and shipping labels, all digital files prepared, a unique hashtag and prompts to get people talking, and blog posts and emails at the ready.

How much ammunition will it take to hold down the territory?

With over 2,000 copies sold before launch, I'll need to give people good reason to keep talking about the book all season long. I'll do sampler blog posts, giveaway contests, interview requests, regular emails, and social media advertising campaigns to keep its momentum going.

What will you do to reinforce and defend your position?

I'll share testimonials and reviews throughout *Your Best Year* season, making sure to showcase real results online entrepreneurs are creating.

Now, it's your turn. Think about an upcoming product or promotion (your next big money maker), and answer the following.

 WHAT'S THE PRODUCT AND WHO IS IT FOR?

 WHO ARE THE TROOPS THAT WILL HELP SUSTAIN IT?

 WHAT SUPPLIES DO YOU NEED TO MAKE THE CAMPAIGN WORK?

HOW MUCH AMMO WILL IT TAKE TO HOLD THE TERRITORY?

 WHAT WILL YOU DO TO REINFORCE YOUR POSITION?

Here is another valuable quote from Grant Cordone's *10X Rule*, a book I would highly recommend every online entrepreneur read for themselves:

"I don't care if your product costs nothing to make and it's 100 times superior to its closest competitor; you will still have to apply 10 times more effort just to push through all the noise in order to get people to even know about it. Assume that every project you attempt will take more time, money, energy, effort, and people than you can imagine."

He advises that you not try to compete in the space, but become it. "The message you want to send to the marketplace through your persistent action is, 'No one can keep up with me. I'm not going away. I am not a competitor. I am *the space*.'"

 A shining example of this is Luminaries Club member, Kara Benz—whom Luminaries will recognize from the masterclass she taught, "Zero to 30K Instagram Followers" inside the club. She came onto the scene with a bullet journal and a blog (found at bohoberry.com), and as soon as she struck such an authentic chord for both herself and her audience, she *became* that space. The creator of the bullet journal even thanked her for the awareness she brought to the planner community!

Her level of action was so persistent, she put in a level of work that no one else was willing to do, and there was no question who came to mind first in her sector. Because of that, Kara's results have been off-the-charts phenomenal.

Chapter 8

BUILD A MARKETING CAMPAIGN

Next I'm going to show you how to build your own marketing campaign using two different business models as examples (product- and service-based). Regardless of what you're offering online, I encourage you to read through both as they each offer many takeaways.

Let's start with the basic blueprint you'll need to complete for any promotion or product launch. For every campaign you create, you'll need to name the marketing goal, a deadline (or run dates), potential earnings, advertising budget (where applicable), and strategies you plan to employ for the campaign with dates for each.

Build Your Own Marketing Campaign (Product Example)

Next, I'm going to fill in the campaign blueprint using examples from my own business. I'll start with my best-selling product promotion, the Friday before Black Friday Sale.

For this promotion, I offered a 40% discount (wholesale pricing). It was always my most anticipated sale of the year. Here is how I ran the four-day deal:

Thursday Night

The customers on my email list get an exclusive invitation. Since stock is limited, my list gets first dibs. I make sure to let them know that they're getting the coupon code early, urging them to get a jump on the crowd.

MARKETING GOAL:

BY:

POTENTIAL EARNINGS:

MARKETING BUDGET:

STRATEGY: **DATE:**

Which platforms will you promote on?   *And when?*
How many times will you email?
Where will you pay to promote?
How much of the budget will you allot to each paid promotion?
What enticing opt-ins will you offer?
What type of teasers will you reveal?
How might you upsell other products/offers?
How will you add scarcity (why buy now?) to the campaign?

List all the places and the different ways you'll promote, and assign dates to each idea.

TASKS:
What do you need to build, do, learn, or acquire in order to make this campaign a success?

Friday before Black Friday

I publicly announce the coupon code via social media. In the past, I've spent anywhere from $20-300 promoting the sale on Facebook.

Saturday

On Saturday, I begin a barrage of "last chance" reminder announcements. They will run at scheduled intervals for all social media channels (every four to six hours). I also send a Saturday morning email that highlights remaining stock and reminds customers that there is only one day left to take advantage of this sale price, while supplies last.

Sunday

I schedule an "Hours Left!" email reminding customers to take advantage of their coupon before it expires.

This campaign was repeated every year, and its success only grew over time. This book is focused on low-cost/no-cost marketing strategies, so in the following examples, I keep the advertising costs low. However, my Friday before Black Friday strategy had absolutely proven itself over time, which would make it a safe bet for investing.

Now that I've told you how the sale runs, I'll show you where it starts and how I brainstorm different ways to get (and keep) my brand on everyone's radar throughout the promotion.

MARKETING GOAL:

150 sales

BY: *November 20*

POTENTIAL EARNINGS:

$3,000

MARKETING BUDGET:

List-based promo

STRATEGY:	DATE:
Share growing inventory pictures on Instagram	*Nov 2—16*
Pre-sale buzz (highlight products) on Facebook	*Nov 14—16*
Pin largely-stocked products hourly to group boards	*Nov 10—24*
Heavy opt-in push, social profile links = "Be on my list!"	*Nov 11—16*
Email early-bird special	*Nov 17*
Sale announcement > all social media accounts	*Nov 18*
Low inventory alerts > Facebook/Instagram	*as needed*
Email reminder highlighting available stock and low inventory alerts	*Nov 19*
Update website/renew listings	*as needed*
Last chance email	*Nov 20*
"Last call for savings!" > all social media accounts	*Nov 20*

TASKS:
Have stock ready to be photographed late October. Design branded opt-in page and shorten link for upcoming promotion (social profiles, updates, etc.). Schedule pins to group boards (Postcron).

For products, I use a sales number versus a dollar amount for the marketing goal simply because there are a range of pricing options. My average sale at the Energy Shop was $20, so I'm aiming for 150 sales or $3,000.

Just setting the marketing goal for my upcoming promotion was always an eye-opener because the product was handmade. I usually didn't have this much in stock, which told me what to focus on months in advance of the sale itself.

With a product-based business, you don't want to promote sales too early. Doing so will stall regular-price sales for the month leading up to the promotion. However, you will want to highlight new products and the inventory you're accruing.

Focus your pre-sale promotions on "get on my list" campaigns, not upcoming sales dates and information. The biggest percentage of sales conversions will happen via email, every time! Change all of your social media profile links to opt-in forms. Make sure every anticipatory post you create gives potential customers a good reason to subscribe to your email broadcasts.

You can come up with a lot of ways to entice them:

- Sign up for my list for an extra 10% off sale prices!
- Email subscribers get first dibs on available inventory!
- Join the pre-party and get email-only early-bird access!
- Subscribe now for exclusive bonuses (email only)!
- Sign up to receive private training and introductory offers not available anywhere else!

If it seems like I'm excited about these offers (!), it's because you have to be as enthusiastic in your marketing of free product as you do in marketing for paid product.

Present everything in a way that moves the relationship forward, as if it's a VIP invitation to the most exclusive event in town. If you're not excited about it, they're going to pass. They're already being bombarded by SPAM, everyday promotions (hello, old faithful 10% off), and desperate pleas for their business.

Now that you've used your upcoming promotion to beef up your email list (growth), it's time to actually host the sale itself (profit). For the Friday before Black Friday Sale, I activated the customer's coupon code on Thursday and distributed it privately via my email list.

I've since dubbed that announcement the "$1,000 email" because it always generated at least $1K the day it was sent. I edited the same email several times a year (changing only the seasonal greeting, coupon code, and dates) for whatever promotion I was marketing.

My sales strategies are always about serving and delighting the customer; I never want anyone who buys from or hires me to feel like prospects. You'll notice that the following script sells without making people feel "sold to." In fact, this email makes my customers reply and leave notes on their order saying, "Thank you so much!"

Let's break it down. I'll show you exactly what I write, and then I'll explain why it works.

Dear friends of the Energy Shop,

I hope this email finds you cozying up in your own personal winter wonderland because ... *It's the most wonderful sale of the year!*

As a thank you for being part of my mailing list, here's YOUR exclusive preview to tomorrow's big sale. Many items in stock are limited edition, and as always, you get first dibs! Come see what's new at the Energy Shop and enjoy ...

40% OFF YOUR ENTIRE PURCHASE
USE COUPON CODE:
THANKSGIVING

It opens to the public tomorrow [Friday, date] and ends on Sunday [date, time, and time zone]. And this is your exclusive invitation to browse the collection before the madness begins!

Happy shopping! As always (and forevermore), I love and appreciate your business.

- Lisa Jacobs

The format is always the same while the details are changed ever so slightly (depending on the season or occasion). It's exciting, and in following with good copywriting format, it's shared not as a sales pitch, but in the spirit of ...

BIG NEWS YOU CAN HARDLY WAIT TO TELL A FRIEND!

It's casual, short, and to-the-point. Anytime you're having a sales conversation with your customers, you will not use the formal writing style you learned in school. Instead, it's the writing you used when you wrote an exciting and secretive note to a friend.

Let's take this email apart and examine why it works so well. It opens with a seasonal image (Friday before Black Friday Sale would be holiday-themed) with an eye-catching subject line. In this case it was, "It's the MOST Wonderful Sale of the Year!"

Next, personalize the email. I didn't collect first names when I started the Energy Shop's email list, and that's a mistake I was sure never to repeat. I prefer to open an email with "Dear [contact.first.name]," (all email management providers will have a different insert for this). But in order to collect your potential customers' first names, your opt-in form has to have it as a required field.

To keep this email personal sans everyone's first names, I use "friends of the Energy Shop." You want to write something beyond just the greeting (Hi, [friends, knit lovers, creatives, fashionistas, forever home shoppers, business builders, designers, etc.]), but where possible, use their actual name.

The warm greeting was followed by:

As a thank you for being part of my mailing list, here's YOUR exclusive preview to tomorrow's big sale. Many items in stock are limited edition, and as always, you get first dibs! Come see what's new at the Energy Shop and enjoy 40% off.

There's actually a lot going on in the above paragraph. It reaffirms the customer's exclusivity with my brand, adds a time frame, and reminds them of the scarcity of my products. And if you read between the lines ("tomorrow's big sale", "first dibs", and later, "before the madness begins") it adds a layer of excitement that builds social proof.

This $1,000 email script practically guaranteed that I would nearly sell out before the public sale even began.

While the actual sale theoretically runs November 18-20, the pre-sale announcement sent on Thursday (November 17) will generate at least 80% of this promotion's revenue. The second best-selling day will be November 20, when the "last chance" email is sent.

Reminder emails will feel like overkill. At this point in the campaign, you'll have been talking about your sale nonstop for nearly four days. It will be hard to imagine that anyone could forget, but they can and they have.

In marketing, you're thinking about your campaign all day, every day for weeks leading up to the promotion. Trust that the customer's not thinking about you *nearly as much* as you're thinking about them.

Build Your Own Marketing Campaign (Service Example)

Next I'm going to show you the behind-the-scenes schedule of the launch of my signature course, Complete Copywriting. It is typically open for enrollment for two weeks, and I like to kick off the launch with an exclusive early-bird registration.

You can easily apply this same launch schedule to your next product release or seasonal promotion, and I encourage you to check out my Complete Copywriting course to make the absolute most of your time and efforts around the launch (it's *a lot of work*, you'll want maximal results).

As with the product-based example, I'll first tell you how the launch is organized. Then I'll show you the campaign blueprint where it all starts and how I brainstorm different ways to get (and keep) my brand on everyone's radar throughout the promotion.

Twelve Weeks Before

- **Nail down product details and deliverability.** Whether I'm creating an ongoing course (several modules), a book, or a single class, I organize the details and have a loose outline of the project at least twelve weeks in advance. Here I determine: what type of product it is, what it's going to do for my clients, and how I'm going to deliver it. For this example, the product is an eight module course delivered weekly. Additionally, I hosted two bonus classes live (using private webinar-hosting) to give both myself and the students an inclusive classroom feel.
- **Create a product-oriented opt-in offer.** The first thing I create and promote for a product is the opt-in offer that speaks directly to its ideal students. For Complete Copywriting, I've created a webinar

("Copywriting Secrets of a Six-Figure Business"), a product listing workbook, and a copywriting checklist.

- **Build a marketing campaign.** Now that I know the details and the loose needs of the project (a guesstimate of how much overall work will be involved), I plug launch dates into the campaign blueprint. Be sure to allow yourself an extra two weeks' leeway. Tasks inevitably take longer than you expect.
- **Start course research and build.** I won't be anywhere near final draft of the project at this stage, and I'll be adding finishing details until the last minute. I spend this time up front to ensure my training has the most comprehensive coverage of the topic on the market.

Eight Weeks Before

- **Name a sales goal for the product.** I typically use the number of subscribers on my email list and project a 2% sales conversion, based on that number (for example, if I have 16,000 subscribers, I project 320 sales).
- **Write the sales page.** Right around this time in project production, I'm really excited about the product and the potential impact it holds. It's a golden opportunity to channel my own excitement and write the sales page. Once written, I refer to the sales page throughout the rest of the course build to ensure I'm delivering everything I promised—it almost becomes my "table of contents" for the project.
- **Decide on pricing.** To come up with a fair price for both me and my students, I test my offer's return on investment. For example, I had private clients test the material in my Complete Copywriting course, and they were immediately reporting huge returns. One of my clients made an unexpected $776 in a week by using just one technique in the program. Better still, it was a technique she could easily repeat four times per year. I knew the course had an excellent return on investment.
- **Figure out the potential return on the launch** (a dollar amount, i.e., if 50 people bought it at $99, this launch could be worth $4,950). I'll do this early on to determine whether or not I want to advertise or invest to make a good launch even better. If I do choose to advertise, I promote the opt-in, not the course. In service, I never ask for sales from strangers.

Six Weeks Before

- **Create an editorial calendar based on the topic at hand.** I aim for one blog post per week, but if it was my first launch and/or my list wasn't as established, I'd aim for at least two blog posts per week.
- **Identify the product's narrative.** This is a copywriting technique, and probably more advanced than you'll find in most launches. I like my product launches to deliver extreme value; I want people to love that I'm selling something even if they choose not to buy. Since launches have me talking about one specific topic for more than a month, I try to create an overarching storyline that is useful and engaging. For example, during The Luminaries Club launch, I taught a narrative on gaining exposure for your business (common problems we all face, as well as solutions and techniques to overcome them).
- **Ready the sales page and course distribution.** The last stages of a launch are busy and quite overwhelming. *It's a lot.* The more you have ready, the better off you'll be.
- **Add the finishing touches to the user's experience.** Imagine you just bought the product you plan to sell. Test the flow and delivery—it's important, and it's a nightmare if you don't have all of your ducks in a row beforehand. Work out any kinks as early as possible to save yourself a lot of stress down the road.

Four Weeks Before

- **(Optional) Set up a live webinar.** This was new to me when I launched Complete Copywriting, and if I'm honest, it really pushed me out of my comfort zone. I've taught on CreativeLive and have plenty of experience presenting at other people's webinars, but I'd never self-hosted a live call before. Now several in, my webinars have an average 20% sales conversion! (The full breakdown and setup, plus my webinar template and sales script are all included in my Complete Copywriting course). To host a webinar, you need a host (I use Webinar Ninja), a prepared presentation (I use Keynote and share my screen), and ideally, a moderator (I use my assistant, Jennie Rensink). Plan and prepare your webinar about four weeks out (practice the entire call out loud), but don't announce it until a week before it airs.

- **Write your sales emails.** I email about the new product at least six times in ten days. For this launch, I emailed ten times in twenty-one days. My emails generate the vast majority of my sales (very few people buy expensive programs straight from my blog), and my sales campaigns earn as much as six figures per quarter.

Two Weeks Before

- **Host a webinar.** I teach the masterclass, "Copywriting Secrets of a Six-Figure Business," which includes a pre-order special bundle, and both the replay and offer expire 72 hours later.
- **Launch the course.** The day my product launches, my three-month long campaign comes to an end. This week is spent welcoming new students as the finale of my email sequence rolls out. I remain on standby to answer any last minute questions.

If it looks like a lot, that's because it is. But, the great thing about online business is that everything is repeatable. If you look at the above sequence and take out: the course research, the course build, the opt-in build, the course testing and pricing (but add collecting testimonials), the product's narrative, the sales page, the welcome sequence, the user's experience, the webinar presentation, and the emails you've finished … because they're already written, researched, prepared, and ready! What will that mean for your business and your schedule next year?

For a more visual look at this process, I'll plug it into the marketing campaign blueprint on the following page.

When you combine confidence in your offer with a clear vision for your campaign, you'll always know WHY you are asking, sharing, working, posting, and making. It gives purpose to every hour you spend on your business.

 As a reminder, your marketing campaign must push forward *no matter what*. Notice that every example displays constant motion; that's intentional. Potential customers cannot see what isn't moving, so your promotion needs to progress and take up space.

MARKETING GOAL:

320 sign-ups for Complete Copywriting

BY: *May 29*

POTENTIAL EARNINGS:	MARKETING BUDGET:
$223,040	*List-based promo*

STRATEGY: DATE:

Blog posts with content upgrades (makeover and checklist)	*Mar 2—16*
Regular weekly emails	*throughout*
Weekly blog posts with course updates and opt-in reminders	*Mar 16—launch*
Photos of course build and topic tips > social media accounts	*April 1—launch*
Webinar announcement and opt-in push	*May 4—11*
Email sales campaign (10-part series)	*May 10—24*
Live webinar: Copywriting Secrets of a Six-Figure Business	*May 12*
Launch and open cart	*May 12*
Scheduled social media posts and reminders	*as needed*

TASKS:
Create opt-in offers. Purchase and learn premium opt-in software (LeadPages). Purchase and learn webinar software (Webinar Ninja).

Let's bring this marketing campaign to life one last time before I turn you loose on your own. I'm using my client, Addison of carolinadandy.com, and one of her marketing campaigns as an example.

CAROLINA ❦ DANDY
MONOGRAM SHOP

MARKETING GOAL:

500 sales during the spring product launch

BY: *March 21*

POTENTIAL EARNINGS:

$12,500

MARKETING BUDGET:

$300

STRATEGY:	DATE:
Instagram influencer outreach (offer free product for exposure week of sale)	*Feb 1—14*
Pre-sale buzz (highlight products) on Facebook	*Feb 25—Mar 9*
Pin largely-stocked products hourly to group boards	*Feb 25—Mar 9*
Heavy opt-in push, social profile links = "Be on my list!"	*Mar 1—Mar 15*
Share reminder to Instagram influencers and affiliate coupons distributed	*Mar 11*
Early-bird email coupon	*Mar 18*
Sale announcement > all social media accounts (promote on Facebook for three days)	*Mar 19*
Low inventory alerts > Facebook/Instagram	*as needed*
Email reminder highlighting available stock and low inventory alerts	*Mar 20*
Update website/renew listings	*as needed*
Last chance email	*Mar 22*

TASKS:
Instagram influencer request script written, proofread, and customized for each request.
Facebook and Instagram promotion (ad spend: $100/day for three days of public sale).

BUILD YOUR OWN CAMPAIGN

MARKETING GOAL:

BY:

POTENTIAL EARNINGS:

MARKETING BUDGET:

STRATEGY: DATE:

TASKS:

Chapter 9

MAKE MORE SALES

In order to survive in business, you must become your number one sales person. Your offer needs to be presented with an enthusiasm so contagious, it carries enough momentum to spread across the globe. That excitement cannot be reproduced; it must be created by you.

Moreover, you must take accountability for your own sales record (or lack thereof). If you're not getting any sales, those are the results you created. If you're not getting as many sales as you'd like, those are the results you created. When you do have a winning campaign and enjoy lots of sales, those are the results you've created (*and not some one-off fluke circumstance!*).

Going forward, and in order to get your marketing strategies to work, you'll need to boldly sell like no other in your industry has sold before. You'll need to deploy your campaign like it's a plow, sent to harvest the field you sowed.

It should be part of an always-moving, ever-expanding bigger picture. Imagine a moving train that's consistently on its way to its next stop. In and of itself, the constant movement builds the potential customer's desire for the product and increases the credibility of the brand.

Let's be crystal clear: If you create your first real sales campaign and receive fewer sales than you expect, you will be tempted to throw in the towel. Keep going anyway.

After my sales campaigns, I hear one of two things: "I'm so glad I bought! Totally looking forward to this." Or, "I'm kicking myself for not taking you up on that offer." I wouldn't have it any other way! This is the perfect response to a good campaign, and I'm always sure to follow through on my strategy *no matter what*. Everything you do, say, post, and write online during your sales campaign is in small ways contributing to the sale, if you're doing it right.

Your marketing campaign is building social proof, it's attracting interest, and it's intriguing customers. If you cut a campaign short, "sales" become just another tactic in the daily scramble toolbox.

Trust your offer. There is definitely a pay gap between newbie pricing and veteran pricing. However, the majority of online entrepreneurs wait entirely too long to upgrade to veteran pricing. Don't make the same mistake.

These are just some of the excuses entrepreneurs make to avoid risk:

- I need more experience/research before it will take off.
- I need to sacrifice more time to make it work.
- My brand's not perfect yet, so the rest is all for naught.
- As soon as I get to [X] sales or [X] subscribers, I'll take the next step!

These are all stalls. The longer I made these same excuses, the longer I kept my business in the poor house. You must trust that you can make good money from your business right now.

Make the Ask

Because I don't have to wonder, I know you're still hesitating to ask for the sale. I feel your hesitancy and match your fear 100%, even after seeing amazing results that came directly from asking for sales!

It's not a business until you're unapologetically asking for sales.

During my first real marketing campaign, I asked my email list to join my membership program, The Luminaries Club a total of six times in a 10-day period.

Before that campaign, I had never asked anyone for anything more than twice: one email to announce and one email to remind. But this time, I unapologetically sold my product for six emails in a row.

Here's what happened next:

- I lost an average of 60 subscribers/email (normal rate is about 35/email).
- I received 3 very angry replies that week.
- I doubled the typical number of SPAM complaints (normal rate is 3-5).
- I welcomed hundreds of new clients and earned $28,000 in one week.

Read that series of events carefully because it's something every creative needs to see.

We've all—every single one of us—run up against that mouthy complainer who can't believe the nerve! *"How dare you use my email address to try to sell your product!"* And "sell" reads like it's the dirtiest four-letter word in the dictionary.

And I need you to know that those mouthy complainers are <u>not your customers</u>.

I know my client's value, and they know mine. The people who make noise are merely trying to interrupt that gorgeous exchange, and I won't allow it. Moreover, notice that "they"—the angry people—are only three voices in a crowd of thousands of interested customers.

Yet we allow them to influence! They are the reason you hesitate to ask, which is their point. They make noise because they know it raises doubt. Those three people were angry before they found me, and they're still somewhere being angry right now!

I need you to hear that, so you'll stop hearing their noise once and for all.

The first time you run a campaign to a list that's not used to you making the ask, expect some kickback. You've taught your subscribers how to treat you, and if you haven't been asking for sales, you haven't taught them you mean business yet.

If you run a series of emails asking for a sale, a few subscribers will protest. That's okay; remember, they're not your paying customers *and they never will be*. It will still make you timid, but you'll know to push through it.

Most potential customers are immobile due to an overwhelming sense of inertia and indecision. Hearing about the product in casual passing will only prompt a few sales, if that. Most sellers let that be their sales pitch for the day and move on, which means, before they've even gotten to the most critical part of the sales campaign, they've already given up.

Don't be one of them!

Instead, I want you to address the customer's hesitation, continue to press the offer, and keep giving them a good answer to the question, "Why buy now?" Yet at the same time, I've told you not to be pushy. What a tightrope to walk, now go! (*Just kidding.*)

Chapter 10

ADDRESS THEIR HESITATION

In order to make a sales campaign feel good for everyone involved, let's look at what's holding your potential customer back. As always, when you know and understand your ideal customer, you can approach them in a very comfortable (read: non-threatening) way. You can address their interests and obstacles in a conversational manner to ensure a positive outcome.

Before any customer makes a purchase, they're thinking …

- What am I going to do with this product if I buy it?
- Am I going to get what I'm expecting, or will I be disappointed?
- Will I be happy owning it?
- What if I'm not happy with it?
- Is it worth the asking price?

As buyers in general, before any of us agree to a transaction, we weigh the pros and cons of the exchange. Here's the kicker: it's human nature to put more value on what we're going to *lose* and less value on what we're going to *gain*.

Therefore, buyers instinctively spend more energy trying to preserve what they already have (their money). When they think about the purchase with a two-million-year-old organ that's been programmed to survive (the brain), their natural reaction is to keep stock and preserve.

It doesn't matter what you're selling. It doesn't even matter if your product will make them more of the money they're protecting! That's simply how the brain works.

All of their hesitation boils down to these two questions:

1. Am I willing to *lose*?
2. Is the potential gain worth the risk?

As a seller, to respect this natural hesitation is one of the most caring things you can do for your potential customers. You can guide them through the transaction, reaffirming along the way that your offer is simply a choice (not a threat or force against them) and the decision is theirs. The last thing that the customer wants is to regret the purchase.

I know I've explained tricks of the trade, such as injecting scarcity into an offer, but they are not meant to manipulate. It's simply an answer to the question, "Why buy now?" It doesn't threaten the customer's survival instincts (as that two million-year old organ chants, "preserve! preserve! preserve!"), but it will help an interested customer breakthrough their own inertia and get them over the hump of indecision.

To really make the most of an offer and help interested customer's overcome their natural hesitation, let's look at three things that are holding them back.

#1 They're Skeptical

If a potential customer is following your brand, it's because they think you have a solution to one of their life's challenges. The customer has a need, whether it be bookkeeping services or a soft t-shirt with the perfect neckline, and they're tuned into your brand because they think you can fill it.

Ideally, they'd like to answer this search once and for all. They're skeptical if you can solve it, but please don't take that intel and run. Sometimes in trying to erase skepticism, online sellers create more doubt. They over explain. They use very technical terms to describe the process of creation. In essence, they try too hard.

Credibility is won with a strong brand statement or customer satisfaction guarantee that alleviates the customer's fear of experiencing buyer's remorse. Here's my example:

In business, you are always going to have more questions. As a Luminary, you'll always know where to turn. The Luminaries Club is full of the help you need … *if you're ready to make the commitment.*

I have a 60-day money-back guarantee. You just have to show me two months' worth of completed coursework (proof that you gave my system a go), and I'll happily refund your money if my training hasn't improved your results.

#2 They're Unfamiliar

There's a psychological phenomenon called the "ambiguity effect" which causes humans to give bias to what is already known. In other words, when presented with a decision, we will choose what is known and predictable over what is new and unfamiliar every time. *Even when what is unfamiliar is the better option.*

What is unknown and unpredictable causes discomfort, even though it hasn't been experienced yet. The mere thought of something causing us discomfort is enough to make us avoid it altogether.

For example, when you're really hungry, you're going to choose a restaurant you know you like rather than visit an unfamiliar one at random. The unfamiliar option could very well be your new favorite of all time, but it also has the potential to cause discomfort by not being the flavor or quality you crave. Therefore, you'll avoid it and stick to what you know.

If a potential customer is thinking about purchasing from you for the first time, their unfamiliarity will be your biggest obstacle. That's why it's so important to present your offer (and expertise) in a language that meets them at their level of understanding.

If you overwhelm a new customer with vague concepts, too many options to choose from, or a very technical language they can't comprehend, you'll lose them forever. To overcome this obstacle, always present your marketing materials in a way that would make sense to someone who just heard of you this morning. Keep the presentation simple, add visuals that help summarize the offer, and make the decision process quick, easy, and convenient.

For example, the banner ad on the following page helped me attract new customers who were unfamiliar with my annual workbook, *Your Best Year* and achieved a 10% sales conversion at once.

THERE'S A BETTER WAY TO PLAN.

{ 2016 }
YOUR BEST YEAR

from:
Lisa Jacobs

A PRODUCTIVITY WORKBOOK
& CREATIVE BUSINESS PLANNER

{ 2016 }
YOUR BEST YEAR

TRY IT FOR FREE!

#3 They're Unsure

We already know the customer's inertia is against you, but there's more. They're also battling an internal "someday syndrome," involving this formula: "I want X, but first I need Y." For example,

- I want that expensive pair of jeans, but first I need to lose five pounds.
- I want to invest in business training, but first I need to make some money.
- I want to take advantage of this sale, but first I need to talk to my husband.
- I want to purchase professional head shots, but first I need a good stylist.
- I want to run a sales campaign, but first I need a better brand!

In other words, the customer always has a way to interrupt their own decision. This hesitation is the easiest to overcome, and the most fleeting of all three. Here, they simply need more time. They're essentially saying "maybe, but maybe not right now." And if you have a good enough reason they should buy now, they'll take the plunge.

However, if your campaign isn't confident and convincing enough, this hesitation quickly becomes a danger zone, a purgatory of indecision.

MARKETING PLAYBOOK *by lisa jacoby*

At this stage, the customer has already overcome their two biggest doubts, skepticism and unfamiliarity. If you allow them, potential customers will exist with "someday syndrome" for so long, they'll forget about you and your product altogether. You risk becoming white noise, and eventually they'll tune you out.

You'll know this rule if you keep online wish lists. My own are full of products I desired at one time, but are now completely overlooked. You don't want that to happen to your offer! In every marketing campaign you create, always incorporate answers to these fundamental questions:

- What's in it for me?
- Why buy now?

In Summary

I've met too many creatives that cringe at the idea of sales, but I'm here to assure you that, when done well, the sale is a soulful act for both the buyer and seller.

A good sales campaign is never about badgering your potential customers; that's what the starving artist would do. They'd struggle to find the customers, bug them mercilessly for business, and should it actually work and someone feel pressured into a sale, more likely than not, they'll be issuing a lot of refunds thanks to buyer's remorse.

Forcefully pushing a sale will ruin long-term relationships. In order to build a strong, healthy relationship with a potential customer, they must feel comfortable and at ease. You must be a choice that they make, and for everyone's sake, you need them to feel good about it.

In general, people over-explain and under-sell. You may think you need a big complex approach, when what you really need is to politely present the same simple content a lot of times in a casual (non-threatening) way.

The better you are at selling, the faster your business will grow. It's a technique to be learned, and if there's ever been a time to learn how to sell more effectively, it's now.

Simply put, the customer wants you to be on top of your sales game. There are no "participation trophies" in sales, same way there's no crying in baseball. Do not passively compete in *any* aspect of business (or *life*, for that matter).

Your customer is not going to feed a starving artist's desperation. They want you to be moving so fast that they have to race to catch up! They want you to be bold and beautiful. They want you to command attention for your talents.

Most of all, they want you to powerfully present the offer that wins their business. They want to feel proud when they take you up on that offer because they want to leave feeling better than before.

Your persistent action and consistent movement will intrigue your customer, and it becomes a long-term commitment for you both. The bond between you and your customers cannot be rushed or pretended; it only works with real ingredients, like a home-cooked meal.

If you find yourself waiting around for things to happen, you've created a deadlock; you're adding your inertia to the customer's and compounding the standstill. They're waiting for something that interests them, and it's your job to show up and present that.

Chapter 11

SELF-CRITIQUE YOUR SYSTEM

Step 1: The Customer's Approach

This set of six questions is considered from the customer's perspective. Most of these ask you to put yourself in the customer's shoes, and you'll want to perform this part of the self-critique by thinking about what they want (not what you think they need) from your product.

#1 Who is the perfect customer for my product?

There are two things in business that I don't give specific guidance on, and those are: your schedule and your ideal customer. These two topics are actually quite customized to suit you, and I don't like to generalize the process by trying to guide everyone to a generic conclusion.

In the beginning, creating an ideal customer is a lot of guesswork, but the profile becomes real and useful over time. If you don't have a detailed perfect customer in mind, you need one. There's an exercise to get you started in the **appendix** of this book.

You simply can't craft an effective marketing system without this profile. Here is a list of characteristics my ideal client holds:

- She has an online presence (be it shop, website, or blog), and she's on the build.
- She's looking to improve her operation.

- She is down to earth with a realistic outlook and work ethic.
- She prefers action over excuses.
- She loves a good brain dump with someone who speaks the industry's language.
- She's not afraid of obstacles, in fact, she welcomes the next.
- She is always ready to take things to the next level.
- She appreciates a well-strategized plan of action.
- She is open-minded, but has her own vision of success.
- She is optimistic with an "anything's possible" outlook.
- She appreciates direct and honest feedback.
- She sees the value in hiring other professionals.
- She likes to surround herself with the best.
- She likes to win.
- She's willing to both showcase her talents and strengthen her weaknesses.

#2 How do people typically find products like mine?

Sometimes entrepreneurs get so comfortable in their niche that they forget what it was like *not* to know everything there is to know about it. You build a marketing system from the level you're at versus the level where you started from (where your customers are likely hanging out).

Go back to the basics of your offer. Where did you start? Where did you first look to know more about the product you are now selling?

It's very interesting how we, as consumers, search for a new product online. Depending on what you're searching for, you probably go straight to one of the following sites to find out more: Etsy, Amazon, Ebay, Pinterest, Google, etc. You go directly to specific sources with an intention to find certain products.

For example, if I were looking for a unique notebook that's not sold in local stores, I'd open Amazon and search for the specific product. I wouldn't use Google as my search engine, I'd start with Amazon (the shopping site *becomes* the search engine).

Where does an interested customer start when they are looking for your offer? Which terms do they search? What website are they likely to use as a search engine?

We go to Etsy when we're looking for a unique touch, Amazon when we're looking for a lot of choices and something we might not find in a regular store, Ebay when we're looking for the best deal, Pinterest when we're looking for examples of style, and Google when it's a specific or uncommon product we don't know much about.

All considered, are you focused on the right search engine for your product?

#3 What's in it for them?

What you think your customer needs and what your customer actually wants are often two very different things. Moreover, I catch most businesses being more concerned about what they want to sell than they are interested in what the customer wants to buy.

Hone in on what it is you have to offer your ideal customer. Think of your customer's needs: whether you fill a void in their life by offering information or inspiration, make their house feel more special by creating home decor they love and adore, or make them feel more complete and confident by giving them that one special accessory for their outfit. There is a purpose for your product in the customer's life, and it's your job to clearly identify it.

#4 What makes me the best person for the job?

In this industry, many people get caught up in the comparison game and feel threatened by competition. That's why a little time and care spent on this question can go a long way. Identifying *why* you're the best person to serve your specific ideal customer is the antidote to scarcity thought and insecurities.

Picture your ideal customer from question one. What makes you the best person for them to buy from? That then becomes your tagline, and should be incorporated into your about page and listings (where applicable).

#5 What makes my customer want to buy?

I could live here all day. I love looking at what makes customers buy, what makes me buy, and why we make those decisions when we do.

What makes people buy? Desire. This is where your customer's internal buying thermometer comes into play. Everything you do online either warms your customer towards the sale (builds their desire) or turns them off (diminishes their desire).

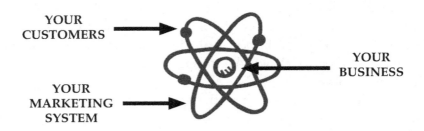

YOUR
CUSTOMERS

YOUR
BUSINESS

YOUR
MARKETING
SYSTEM

Your constant motion, your appeal to their interests, and the patient strategy within your marketing system is what will make your ideal customer take the leap and populate your business.

#6 How will you WOW them?

Give those customers a reason to return! Offer them a discount, send them a surprise bonus, upgrade their purchase, or include free shipping. *Whatever it takes.* Continuously think of new ways you can surprise customers, new and old alike. The extra mile is always worth it.

Now it's time to self-critique your marketing system ...

Step 2: The Marketing System

This set of five questions is considered from your marketing standpoint.

#1 Where are you currently <u>reaching</u> for new customers?

And don't start rattling off all of the social media platforms where you're wasting your time! I want to know where you're reaching AND successfully connecting with your potential customers.

If you're using Twitter and sharing random thoughts and product listings to a following you've doctored (#followback), you're not reaching potential customers. If you're posting on Facebook to zero likes or comments, you're not reaching potential customers. If you're pinning on Pinterest with no repins, hearts, or comments, then you're not reaching potential customers!

For example and until recently, the only place I actively reached my potential clients was Pinterest. I was using Facebook and Twitter regularly, but I was rarely connecting on those platforms.

I was about to give up on Facebook, until I changed the way I was using it.

I decided to create and manage a free-to-join group where my potential clients could boost their marketing efforts. My Facebook connection is now through the roof.

Where are you not only reaching, but connecting? How might your efforts on the non-working social media platforms be altered to reach and connect with your potential customers? (And if nothing works on a specific platform, don't waste your working hours there any longer!)

#2 How are you engaging your potential customers?

If someone takes interest in your business, let's say they decided to follow you on Facebook, be very careful that your posts are written to engage their interest and not just promote your product.

I love the way my client, Nalana of bookscentscandles.com, engages her Facebook audience. She makes candles inspired by best-selling novels with scents to enhance the stories you love. Her social media posts reminisce over fictional characters while introducing inspired scents. It's brilliant! There's dimension and mutual interest in her conversations; it is engagement at its finest.

When engaging, avoid calling potential customers "fans" or "followers." It creates a false belief that the people who have taken interest in your business are overtly interested in you and your life. They're not. They're selfish, as we all are, and they're still very much only thinking of themselves.

Once a potential customer has connected with you, it's your opportunity to keep the conversation going, but you must do that in a way that's interesting to them.

#3 How are you establishing trust?

When I meet a potential customer, let's say they just found my article on Pinterest, I am not asking for the sale. That honestly wouldn't be good for either of us. Rather, I spend a lot of time subtly asking: Am I providing you with valuable information? And if so, are my services a good fit for your business?

As a result, my paying clients truly trust me. I wouldn't have it any other way.

99

#4 How are you converting sales?

I am dumbfounded when product-based business owners tell me how much stuffing their listing titles with every keyword imaginable has helped their views. *Dumbfounded*, I tell you! So your views increased when you stuffed your titles full of every keyword imaginable? *Yeah? Then what happened?*

"Not everything that can be counted counts, and not everything that counts can be counted."—Albert Einstein.

A good marketing system doesn't result in *views*, it results in *sales*. But, I digress. The best place to have a sales conversation with your customers is via email. Make sure you have email campaigns planned and scheduled throughout the year to ensure profit.

#5 How are you following up and building relationships?

A sales funnel is a cycle that repeats itself. Meaning, it's set up so that your customers can go back through it again and again (versus a one-off sale). What are you doing to increase customer lifetime value and keep your existing customer's attention.

In Closing

The strategies you've created for yourself throughout this book are what's required for your personal vision of success. The journey ahead of you is not the easiest choice, I assure you. I applaud your commitment and thank you for your courage and service! Your passion makes the whole world come more alive.

Should you ever feel like giving up, consider this story from *Think and Grow Rich*. Napolean Hill wrote of R.U. Darby, who invested in mining during the gold-rush days. He and his uncle had discovered an ore of gold and bought the equipment they needed to mine the land. As soon as they began drilling below the ore, they found that the vein of gold disappeared completely! They kept drilling to no avail, until they finally gave up hope and quit.

Mr. Darby sold the machinery to a junk man for a fraction of its cost. The junk man then called a mining engineer to evaluate the land, and the engineer calculated that the vein of gold would be found three feet from where Mr.

Darby and his uncle had stopped drilling. When Mr. Darby quit, he was three feet away from striking millions of dollars worth of gold.

"Most great people have attained their greatest success just one step beyond their greatest failure."—Napoleon Hill

Your success awaits, and I'm rooting for you every step of the way. If you should need anything, find me at marketyourcreativity.com.

My team and I would love the privilege of working with you further, whether you sign up for my weekly newsletter, decide to join us in the Luminaries Club, or meet up at our next live event, I look forward to watching your business grow.

Cheers to your most profitable years,

—lisa jacobs

GLOSSARY OF TERMS

We're going to sort through some commonly used terms often found in marketing books, and I should know; I've studied them all. I'm including this glossary to make this as comprehensive a resource as possible. Without directly naming these terms, I've incorporated most of this knowledge into the systems and strategies I shared in *Marketing Playbook*.

call to action—In copywriting, these are words that elicit a response and inject urgency. Essentially, the call to action tells the visitor exactly what to do next. Examples are: "buy now," "sign up today," and "click here."

competition—Contrary to popular belief, a saturated market is a good thing! It means there's already a high demand for your offer. The key to overcoming an overcrowded market is learning how to market outside of it. Don't think of yourself as one in a million, but rather an industry that billions of people don't yet know about.

Imagine this: If you could figure out how to tell everyone in the entire world about your product right now, and then weed out the people who were interested from the people who were not, you would never be able to keep up with the demand from those who were interested. Not by yourself, anyway.

Learn to use the competition to your advantage by identifying some role model businesses.

See also: role model business, human inertia

copycats—Market research is good. Competitor-stalking is a waste of time, and that's where copycats and the fear of them tend to creep in.

I'm skeptical of copycat accusations, and I feel myself cringing at anyone who throws that word around. Don't claim you're the victim unless you're willing to admit that you're sometimes also the culprit! Unless of course, you've completely barricaded yourself indoors with nothing but your imagination and a blank canvas.

We're all inspired by the word and work of others, but in my experience coaching entrepreneurs, the concept of copycatting appears in two forms: (1) The basic fear of "not being original enough." In other words, "I might create something that accidentally resembles another product I've seen in my lifetime!" Or, (2) the debatable idea that they're "too original" and everyone will try to steal their work. In other words, "Everything I do is so unique, and everybody wants to steal my ideas!"

Either way, here's how to fix the issue: stick to the facts.

- You don't have to strive to be unique; you already are.
- You don't have to protect your uniqueness; no one can take it from you.
- You know how to tap into your imagination and create something from nothing. That's amazing; never fear showing it off!
- You are passionate (and possibly somewhat of a perfectionist) which means you pour your heart and soul into your creation. No one could replicate or replace that, no matter what.
- Your creations reflect what is beautiful to you; it's a form of innovative self-expression and cannot be copied.
- Even if another professional, artist, maker, or designer has created something similar at one time or another, their work can never be exactly like yours. Yours is authentic.

I know that there are horrible copycat stories circling the web in which beautiful artwork was copied or plagiarized or boxed in a big store. Hands down, those are crimes against the artist. However, those stories are not the norm.

In online business, we're making it all up as we go along. When we come to depend on this income and our livelihood is at stake, scary stories like those create widespread panic, and I'm no fan of panic.

You don't have to be afraid of copycats. I'm telling you this from experience. Sure, it can happen, but it's very unlikely that it will matter to your bottom line. The shocking truth about copycats is that they'll either be forced to carve their own path or shrivel in someone else's shadow.

As an entrepreneur, it's your nature to observe the world (and other creators) around you. In doing so, you often find new inspiration. Don't let this scare you … it doesn't mean you're copying or vulnerable to being copied. Observing the beauty around you only means you're awake, alive, and well. Breathe it in and continue to be inspired.

See also: human inertia

customer lifetime value—It's essential to know how much a new customer is worth to your business' bottom line throughout the lifetime of the business relationship. For every customer you retain, how much business profit can you predict? Or another way to calculate it is: What is the average profit gained from your existing client base?

The very next question to ask: How can you increase the profit *and* expand the relationship between you and your customers? Customer lifetime value is as much about creating mutually beneficial long-term relationships between you and the client as it is about bringing more profit to your business.

customer relationship management (CRM)—In some of my advanced training, I get into customer relationship management and software (Infusionsoft, Convert Kit, and Salesforce are examples of CRM software). This is the next level to email management, and I would highly recommend it to information- or service-based businesses with an email list of 10,000 or more subscribers.

Essentially, customer relationship management means segmenting your potential customers into specific topic or level of interest. With Infusionsoft (my software of choice), I can track each subscriber's level of interest (based on how often they open and click within my emails), apply tags to their account (based on the specific links they click), and send segmented campaigns accordingly.

For example, I offer programs designed for storefront owners (product-based businesses). Approximately 30% of my list own storefronts, which I've segmented based on their articles of interest in my weekly newsletters. Rather than sell my storefront-optimizing programs to the entire list, I can create a campaign that mails only to the 30% who actually need the product.

direct response marketing—This is the style of marketing you use as an online business owner. It allows you to track, measure, and entice a specific (niche) audience. It elicits a direct response to a call to action (e.g., *sign up, click here, buy now*, etc.)

See also: call to action, permission-based marketing

elevator pitch—This is a phrase that prompts you to determine how you'd describe your business or ask for a sale in one or two sentences. Online business owners spend way too much time here. Unless you solicit sales in person and/or to strangers, your elevator pitch will be primarily used to increase your preparedness when asked, "What do you do for a living?"

email marketing provider—If you have yet to start an email list, you need an email marketing service that manages the emails for you. Examples of these are companies like MailChimp, Aweber, Constant Contact, Mad Mimi, and Vertical Response.

Some are free to join, but you'll incur fees as your list grows. Others start at a low monthly rate. This is a non-negotiable expense for your business as it will help you organize, schedule, and deliver your email campaigns. They'll also keep your business compliant (all of these companies are up-to-date with SPAM laws).

*See also: **Appendix***

human inertia—From Google, inertia is "a tendency to do nothing or to remain unchanged."

Instead of competition or copycats, this is where your concern should lie. Rather than shopping with the competition, it is more likely your customer isn't shopping at all.

ideal customer—The ideal customer has many different names in marketing and business. It's also referred to as the "customer profile," "your tribe," "your biggest fan," "customer avatar," and I call mine "dream clients." But, it all means the same thing. The ideal customer is a fictional description of a single person, and that one person represents your entire customer pool. The ideal customer is the sum total of similar traits, hobbies, and interests that your customer base might have in common.

*See also: **Appendix***

permission-based marketing—This is the focus of this book. It means segmenting your ideal customers from non-buyers by focusing on common interests or niche appeal, and then requesting their permission to market to them (aka opt-in).

Today, we are a market made of millions, if not billions, of niche interests. This is fantastic progress for the world, and it's fantastic news for the online business you're building. More than ever, nothing is for everybody ... not that it ever was.

One of my favorite things about marketing these days is not only the customers you can find and retain on your own, but also the opportunities you can seize by building your own niche audience. It eliminates the gate keepers (traditional publishing houses, retail licensing firms, even TV producers). You can create the audience for just about any marketable thing you want to build.

Also known as: interest-based marketing, niche marketing

mass marketing—It used to be that in order to get a consumer's attention, you needed to buy a television commercial, radio commercial, or print advertisement because you had to market to the masses. Businesses had to reach the largest audience possible in order to find their share of interested customers.

We are a mass market no more, and that is the beauty of online business. Because of this new era of individualism, customers have tuned out mass broadcasts. When was the last time you watched a show as it aired (not on demand), and paid attention to the commercials?

Instead, we carefully select who can enter our lives and which products we'll grant our attention. Your customers want to feel the same way you feel: cared for, unique, and important.

role model business— A role model business is a person or corporation that does something similar to what you want to achieve. Your role model has already conquered that which currently overwhelms you, and the answers you seek are readily available with a little reconnaissance.

They are also going to be shining examples of how to turn your product or service into a successful business. When you come across an obstacle while expanding your online presence, you can almost always ask: what would/ does my role model do? Applying their proven techniques to the way your business operates will spark new insights and ideas for growth.

Here is how to find a role model business:

1. Name a few keywords that you associate with your creative business, product, and/or service. Google those keywords to see what businesses appear on the first few pages of search results.
2. Identify at least one go-to big business in your field. You want somebody that is charging a strong price and creating a desirable experience for their customers.
3. Next, analyze what's working about your role model by asking: How do they present their products? What do they call similar products? How do they describe their offer/brand? What are their service policies? What do they do better than you? What do you do better than them? How does their "about" page read?

Bigger businesses often leave their copywriting, marketing, and advertising research right on the table. All you have to do is dig a little deeper, and enjoy the learning curve.

THE CUSTOMER FLOW CHART

sales funnel—A sales funnel is made up of all the landing sites and touch points in which visitors will find you. It's a pipeline that is designed to perpetually attract, interest, convert, and retain new customers.

I demonstrate all sales funnel concepts with the customer flow chart.

social proof—The psychological phenomenon that causes us to like what we perceive as popular. In other words, the best way to get new people to see your work is by having a lot of people already looking at it.

Social proof helps the customer feel "at home" while shopping with you. On Etsy, it's the combination of history and experience (as well as the site-familiarity that Etsy provides) that helps the customer trust the transaction. Social proof can also come from word-of-mouth, product reviews, and brand recognition (e.g., "Oh! I've heard of the Energy Shop before! My best friend LOVES her bracelet.").

You can help your customer find social proof on your business by using phrases such as, "best-selling," "back by popular demand," and "previously sold out" on items that have a history of doing just that. Your customers are influenced by people with similar tastes, and they'll automatically find people with kindred needs in your sales history.

unique selling proposition (USP)— This is a marketing term created to help you position yourself as a stronger option than anyone else on the market.

In other words, why should a customer buy from you over your competitors? Your answer is your USP.

APPENDIX

While easy to understand and implement, the strategies within *Marketing Playbook* are advanced. The material assumes you have an online point of sale, a product for sale, some interested buyers, and an email list manager.

If you are in the researching stages of your business and one or more of these aren't in place yet, I've included instructions on how to achieve them in this section.

 ## IDENTIFY YOUR IDEAL CUSTOMER

If you're at a place in business where you feel as though you're all in—you're putting in the time, energy, and production it takes to build a selling website—but the business isn't giving back (in the form of sales, growth, and revenue), then this ideal customer exercise is going to be your first step in getting on the right track. Are you …

- doing a lot of talking and posting, but feel as though nobody is listening?
- churning out a lot of products, but nobody's buying?
- reaching for customers every way you know how, but connecting with no one?

The general advice for marketing in business is to "write as if you're talking to one person." Right? I've heard that floating around, and I'm sure you have, too. The problem with that advice is that it's incredibly generic.

Imagine I issued you a coaching assignment in which you had to go out all day long and have sales conversations with everyone you encounter. You have to go shopping, grab a coffee, have lunch with an old friend, etc., but you have to be out all day and put yourself in front of a mix of new people.

If you're anything like me, this wouldn't be a comfortable assignment (I'm an introvert through and through), but it would be doable. I would think ahead on every situation and consider HOW I would approach them. At check-out, I might notice the store clerk's jewelry, then offer her a free sample with my business card. I could cut straight to the point with an old friend. Approaching all of these people might not be comfortable for me, but I would work it out.

But what if I layered on that generic advice and told you that you had to speak "as if you're talking to one person," and you had to have the same exact sales conversation with everyone you encountered? I don't know about you, but I'd quit the coaching assignment based on how that would make people feel.

You see, if you're not addressing your customers in a very personal and targeted manner, you make everyone you encounter feel like prospects. And that's never how I want people who hire or buy from me to feel.

You have something valuable for sale. The question becomes: *How do I find the people who value it?* And we don't want just anybody's attention. It's for a select sea of people who share your taste, have an eye for your talents, and love the quality product you produce.

The one thing you MUST DO before attempting any type of marketing is to identify your ideal customer. This is a personal exercise for your business, and one you should take very seriously. I instruct my clients to sit down with pen and paper, and set aside time just to focus on this assignment.

The ideal customer has many different names in marketing and business. It's also referred to as the "customer profile," "customer avatar," and I call mine "dream clients." But, it all means the same thing. The ideal customer is a fictional description of a single person, and that one person represents your entire customer pool. The ideal customer is the sum total of similar traits, hobbies, and interests that your customer base might have in common.

While this person does not actually exist, it can be based on actual customers you've had (or you want). I'm so proud of my clients, and they make me smile for different reasons all of the time. I continuously ask myself: "What attribute, characteristic, or attitude am I loving about this person?"

And then, I add that trait to my ideal customer profile because I want to attract MORE of it in business.

The ideal customer exercise never excludes other shoppers. I hear this concern a lot, as in, "If I'm writing and marketing to a specific person, say a middle-aged women decorating her home, then men or professional interior designers won't want to buy from me." Wrong! In fact, that couldn't be further from the truth.

This exercise does not exclude any customers, but it does make a specific customer feel a deep sense of belonging. When you create that sense of belonging with your ideal customer, everyone feels it. It builds more feelings of belonging and attracts loyalty to your brand.

IDEAL CUSTOMER MOCK-UP

ARE THEY MALE OR FEMALE?   WHAT AGE RANGE (18—24, 25—32, ETC.)?

MARRIED OR SINGLE?   RAISING CHILDREN?

ARE THEY RURAL, URBAN, OR SUBURBAN?

WHAT COUNTRY DO THEY LIVE IN? ARE THEY COASTAL OR LAND-LOCKED?

DO THEY LIVE IN A RENTAL, STARTER HOUSE, OR FOREVER HOME?

WHAT'S THEIR FAVORITE WAY TO      WHAT IS THEIR PERSONAL STYLE?
HAVE FUN?   (BOHO, PREPPY, FEMININE,
                                                            INDUSTRIAL, MASCULINE, ETC.)

WHAT TV SHOWS DO THEY WATCH?

WHAT MAGAZINES AND PODCASTS DO THEY SUBSCRIBE TO?

DO THEY PREFER THE GYM OR GREAT OUTDOORS? WHAT'S THEIR FAVORITE FORM OF EXERCISE?

WHO'S THEIR FAVORITE ACTOR?   NAME SOME OF THEIR FAVORITE BOOKS:

WHAT'S THEIR PERSONALITY LIKE? ADVENTUROUS OR LAID-BACK? HOMEBODY OR SOCIALITE?
SILLY OR SERIOUS? POLITE OR DIRECT?

THE SECRET TO GAINING EXPOSURE

The definition of exposure is "an act or instance of being uncovered or unprotected."[2]

When I tell you that you're going to put yourself out there to gain exposure for your brand, I want you to know that I've been through it and I know what a vulnerable act it is. Marketing and sales excite me, and I want you to be excited about those aspects of your business, too.

However, getting started isn't always easy. It's a leap of faith, and marketing is the act of putting yourself out there in an exposed way. Creatives often post on social media and call it "marketing," but as you now know, that's not enough. It's an involved process.

Posting on social media feels pretty safe to most, but once you add a strategic business plan behind it and commit to doing it in a purposeful and direct way, a deep-seated fear of social rejection creeps in. When we talk about exposure, I'm asking you to face that fear head-on.

It doesn't matter who you are or what type of personality you have, that deep-seated fear is human nature. That's what makes exposure so vulnerable; if everyone knows what you're doing, everyone will know if you fail.

I looked up the definition of "vulnerable,"[3] and these were the options:

- capable of or susceptible to being wounded or hurt, as by a weapon
- open to moral attack, criticism, temptation, etc.
- (of a place) open to assault; difficult to defend

I thought these were each so interesting, but one stood out to me more than any other: "(of a place) open to assault; difficult to defend." The dictionary used "a vulnerable bridge" as an example of the definition. It got me to thinking.

Does a successful online business simply mean crossing the vulnerable bridge between where you are and where you want to be?

And if so, no wonder we build armor around our dreams. Which by the way, is what I used to think I had to do in order to succeed in my creative career. I'm always taking a leap that no one I know has ever taken before, so

---

[2] encyclopedia.com
[3] dictionary.com

each time I share my big dreams, they seem open to assault and difficult to defend. But, it doesn't have to be so scary.

Getting comfortable with exposure is key to any marketing strategy. Because this business is often so personal (you're doing or making something you love), I've heard a lot of online entrepreneurs refer to marketing and selling with negative undertones.

But the way I see it, and if you're going to call this a business, you have to ask somebody for something. You're either going to ask your potential customers to buy the product, or you're going to ask yourself (and possibly your family) to justify a very expensive hobby.

There are three steps to mastering exposure: (1) Get comfortable with exposure; (2) Get comfortable asking for exposure; and (3) Ask for exposure all the time. Let's discuss.

#1 Get Comfortable with Exposure

From where I'm sitting, I can guarantee three things: Your product is personal, your business is passionate, and your perspective is always too close.

Many creative entrepreneurs pursue business with their offer bundled like a newborn baby. It's in their hearts, it's beloved, and it's protected. They've just birthed their new idea, and they don't want it to be judged or criticized.

It took me over a year to tell anyone I knew personally that I was in business. The truth is, I was scared of what a few skeptical friends and family might think of the whole idea. I soon realized that I was waiting for my big break before I shared the news. I wanted something to validate me, to make my business seem worthy and established.

After the first year of business, I decided *no more holding back*. I realized that the people who are doing all the succeeding in life are the people who take chances and giant leaps of faith. I realized the people in my life should build me up, and I was no longer going to settle for anything less.

Since then, I've boldly let everyone know who I am and what I do. I've also made mistakes. I've enjoyed enormous breakthroughs. I've also fallen to my knees and wept at rejection. I've launched products and earned as much as $40,000 in less than a week. I've also put things out into the world that nobody had any interest in, lost money, and wasted resources.

Even if you were my worst critic, would you think me a failure? Of course not! You'd rack it all losses up to lessons learned and experience gained. When I list my biggest failures next to my biggest wins, you see that I'm simply doing what it takes to be a successful entrepreneur.

To have a thriving small business, you have to own it! You have to tell your family and friends about it, and let your passion escape you wherever you go. Business comes with trial and error. You'll experience some rejection along the way, but know this …

It's always a mistake to think you can limit yourself and expand at the same time.

I can't guarantee that every marketing strategy you create will pay out, but I can guarantee that it will be worth it to try.

#2 Get Comfortable Asking for Exposure

We have online business in common, but we are made of many different personalities. My clients are introverts and extroverts alike. Everyone has a comfort zone that needs stretching, and we each have weaknesses to strengthen.

I am an introvert, and nothing about business presentation is comfortable to my personality. But I made an agreement with myself that I would push my comfort zone to a place of constant expansion. I dubbed it the "uncomfortable zone."

You'll know you're here when being uncomfortable becomes sort of comfortable.

When I realized my business was going to call me to present, I knew it was my weakness; I did not yet know how to present myself. Therefore, I trained to become a Zumba instructor. The whole point of it was to learn how to take and own the stage.

I was so scared during the first song I taught as an instructor that I held my breath the entire time. I didn't take up more than four square feet of that stage!

After some practice, a university hired me to teach weekly classes. The fitness manager liked my choreography and ability, but felt my presentation was still lacking. She advised me to take a class from the most popular instructor at the gym, a woman named Natasha, before taking the stage again.

When Natasha took the stage, she owned every square inch! She gave the class big movements, big drama, and big fun. The participants had no time to think let alone feel self-conscious, we all raced to catch up to her level of uninhibited performance.

As a participant watching someone boldly do all of that without an ounce of hesitation? Natasha earned instant credibility. She *belonged* on the stage without question.

As a leader, it's hard to put down all fears of social criticism, rejection, and worrying about what others will think. It's hard to break out and do your own thing. *It's scary to put your cares to the side and just dance.*

What we can all take away from that lesson is this: Going big is expected of you, so you better get comfortable with it. If you're going to step up and take the stage, you better command the room's attention when you get there. It makes everyone else more comfortable when you do.

This is a mindset, and the more comfortable you get in gaining exposure, the more traction your business will gain. That means, without doubt or hesitation, turn your ideas into actual plans and then continually present those plans to others.

#3 Ask for Exposure All the Time

The third and final step is, once you get comfortable asking for exposure, ask for it all the time.

One of the biggest questions I get asked about online business is: "How do I get found?" I love to do a 180-degree spin on that question. If someone looks to me to ask, "How do I get found?" I immediately turn them around to look towards the billions of people on Earth and say, "No. How do YOU find your customers?"

That's the mindset you need to adopt because that's marketing.

It's saying, "Where are you? Because I know there are thousands of you out there right now." It means believing they're looking for you, charging straight toward them, and then positioning yourself directly in their path.

When I was writing my first class on marketing for The Luminaries Club, I came up with forty-two different methods I've used to market to potential customers. Aside from the obvious (social media accounts), I've sent direct mail campaigns, rented booths at local shows, contacted my favorite supply manufacturers to become a brand ambassador, and paid to gift product on the red carpet at the Golden Globes.

I gave myself ten minutes to write that list, and came up with forty-two ways off the top. The truth is, I've tried hundreds of methods to reach my customers over the years. To me, the more important question has always been:

What methods *haven't* I tried to reach new customers?

That's what I'm constantly asking, and that's what I want you to always be asking as well. Exposure isn't easy and it's not always comfortable, but to take this business to the next level, it's still your responsibility.

What is your biggest obstacle in marketing?

Is it not knowing how to connect with your customers? Are you still waiting for sales? Validation? A big break? Does "go big" or "get seen" go against the grain of your personality? Is there some further training or experience you think you need in order to be taken seriously?

Now is the time to identify your limitations. Let's discuss the confidence and commitment you'll need to bring to the stage in order for all of this to work.

If you find yourself saying …

- That works for [you/him/her/them], but I'm different because …
- I don't have …. [what someone else has been building for years, such as an email list, the traffic, the sales, the funds, etc.]
- Someone else has more [training/popularity/experience/recognition] in my space
- We don't market like that in my industry

Stop it. These are justifications you're using to stay exactly where you are, snuggled in your comfort zone. Because you know as well as I do, everyone had a start somewhere.

How are you getting in the way of your own success? What are your go-to limitations?

For example, I wanted to create modern email opt-in landing pages for my blog, and I wanted to use the program called Leadpages to do it. It was an overwhelming obstacle I chased in my mind for months.

My limitations were that it cost money to sign up, and I didn't know how to design a landing page or work the program. After I hurdled those issues, it would take time to build the pages; they'd need copywriting, graphics, email integration, etc.

When I catch myself him-hawing over humps like these in business, I stop to assess the issue by answering the questions below. I find that I've typically done nothing to conquer the issue besides fuss over it.

Then, I make a simple task list like so:

1. Decide which offer to promote on the landing page
2. Prepare that document
3. Sign up for Leadpages
4. Build the first opt-in offer
5. Promote that page

Once I finally simplify the process, the goal (that has often been on my to-do list for months) is complete within a matter of hours. You don't need to know exactly how to do something before you start, but you do need to start.

 WHAT IS ONE THING YOU COULD DO TO BETTER MARKET YOUR BUSINESS, BUT YOU'VE BEEN TOO OVERWHELMED TO TACKLE?

 WHAT ARE THE ACTUAL COST AND TIME REQUIREMENTS?

 WHAT IS STOPPING YOU FROM TACKLING IT RIGHT NOW?

 IS IT TIME TO GO FOR IT? IF NOT NOW, WHEN?

HOW TO START AN EMAIL LIST

Are you ready to grow an email list for your online business? Starting from scratch to build an email list can feel very overwhelming, and I get it. You've already put yourself out there by creating a product and building a sales page. And we all know what the email list is for: direct contact and marketing.

It's another stretch of your comfort zone in an already vulnerable situation.

There are many new questions that come with building an email list, but a high number of interested subscribers practically guarantees success in online business. It's a must.

If I haven't convinced you by now, an email list is mandatory for growth and profit, and I'm determined to get you started today! After all, getting started is the hardest part.

For the Energy Shop, I've found that every email on the subscription list is worth $1 during a promotion. In other words, when there were 250 people on that list, a promotional email with a coupon code inside generated approximately $250 in profit. The same thing happened when there were 500 people on my list, and again when there were 750 people. The dollar amount I profited continued to increase with the number of people who subscribed.

The dollar amount the email earns either exceeds or comes very close to the number of people on the list! That is how valuable each subscriber for your mailing list will be! When I had an excellent month at the Energy Shop it was because I connected with my mailing list subscribers and offered them a special promotion.

Choose an Email Marketing Provider

Running an online business without an email list is the equivalent to building a home without installing the foundation; your efforts are guaranteed to sink!

I have two favorite email managers, MailChimp (a great starter option that's free up to 2,000 subscribers) and AWeber (starts at a low monthly fee), but there are many to choose from. Simply Google "email marketing" for a comprehensive, current list of options.

In this section, I'm going to walk you through the MailChimp sign-up because it's free to open an account and very user-friendly.

1. Visit mailchimp.com
2. Click "Sign Up Free"
3. Enter the email, username, and password you want associated with your new account. Click "Get Started!"
4. Check your email and activate your account
5. Enter your information, press "Save and Get Started"

You have an email list! To create your first opt-in link, choose "Lists" from the navigational menu and name your first email list (this is sometimes displayed to customers, so your name or your business name are good choices).

1. Click "Create List"
2. Enter your list details, and click "Save"
3. You'll be redirected to your first list page (find the name you chose at the top, and a navigational bar below)
4. Click "Signup forms"
5. Click "General forms"
6. Customize and find the signup form URL just above the customizations

You have your first opt-in form!

⭐ HOW TO GROW AN EMAIL LIST

I want to give you three effective strategies to grow your list, but before you embark on these strategies, you will want your opt-in boxes and links everywhere. Here's where you might consider adding them …

- Blog sidebar
- Blog header
- End of blog post
- Link in online storefront description (second paragraph as to not interrupt SEO)
- Facebook tab (get instructions from your email manager)
- Facebook call to action
- Instagram profile
- Share in anticipation of upcoming sale ("Sign up for an email exclusive!")
- Send link with sales order receipt
- Use Hello Bar or similar "pop-up" apps

Here are three effective strategies to help you grow your email list.

#1 Pair Up with the Competition

I have always preferred niche collaboration over competition. It's a waste of energy to rival another business, so my feeling is, let's work together and help each other out!

In the past, the best way to partner up with someone else in your niche was to guest post. The strategy was: I write a high-quality post for your site, and in exchange, you introduce me to your audience. If the guest poster's article was good and the host's audience was large, it was a win-win for everybody.

However, guest-posting is an old-school technique that's become much less effective. It's not the best use of your time, unless you get a spot on one of the major sites in your industry. People rarely click through these days—in order to increase our productivity, we've learned to stop falling down that rabbit hole.

Before I move on to what does work, let me give you a tip on how to determine whether or not guest-posting is a good idea:

1. Open Google Chrome or download it as your internet browser.
2. Grab the Alexa browser extension. (All of this is free.)
3. Use Alexa to rank your site alongside some comparable sites in the industry.
4. Offer guest posts to the most popular.
5. Be sure to give readers a reason to click back to your site.

Most sites will allow you to leave a link in your bio (at the end of the post), but you need more than that to get readers to click through. You either need to leave an offer somewhere within the article (such as, "click here to download my full report on the subject") or use your website as an example in the post.

One of the founding members of The Luminaries Club, Lorena of haldecraft.com shared a guest post about Etsy alternatives on my blog and used her website as an example of what Shopify can do. It went on to become one of my most popular posts and still earns her many click-throughs today.

Host an online conference for your industry or ideal customers. I've taken part in many conferences and summits like this, and you may even consider creating one yourself. Industry experts are gathered and interviewed (it involves about a one hour investment of time on everyone but the organizer's part). Each speaker shares the conference with their list which, in turn, introduces that list to all of the other speakers at the event.

There's also the potential to earn money by selling tickets and offering an affiliate program to all speakers involved (this helps them get a kick-back, giving them more incentive to share).

Create a gift guide. The potential for this hit me back in 2011 when one of my favorite Etsy sellers emailed her list a promotion ... for other creative businesses! She sent a gift list full of all the other handmade artists she was buying that year, thereby introducing new makers to her audience.

If you collaborated with a few complimentary products in the industry and agreed to share their products with your list in exchange for them sharing yours with theirs, there's no limit to how many people you could reach!

Teach what you know. If you make a product, don't forget the teaching side of the business as well! A how-to book might take one person months, but how fun would a knitting book with a different technique from all their favorite sellers be to organize and create? Everyone would write a segment, and the person who puts it all together gets special credits and props from all contributors.

#2 Scratch an Itch

In this strategy, you want to dismantle your ideal customer's main problem or pain point with an actionable, easy-to-implement solution. And then give it away for free. This can be as simple as a one-page cheat sheet (a summary or informational guide to your product) or as involved as an e-book, but it's got to be good.

If you're selling something that doesn't involve a whole lot of information (fashion jewelry, for example), an enticing discount on the customer's first sale works well too. I like a 20% off your first order deal (with sign-up to email) or a $50 off a more valuable product (something that's $200 or more).

And by the way, I always give this advice after I've shown how valuable an email list actually is. Remember the $1,000 email? I run that campaign several times per year. When sellers hear "discount" or "coupon," they think: LOSS! But, that's just not the case. Small businesses know that finding new customers is much more expensive than keeping them satisfied (through repeat business).

So if the offer cuts into your profits on that first sale a little bit, chalk it up as marketing expenses well-invested and ensure that customer will want to come back for more!

In either case, let's be crystal clear. The offer you create is guaranteed to cost you in either time or money because you need to give potential customers a very good reason to pick you out of millions of online sellers. It'll be worth the initial investment.

Example offers:

- A discount or coupon
- An informational guide your customer can use (for example, I could offer a crystal meaning and care guide to Energy Shop customers)
- A list of resources, such as my "Little Black Book for Online Businesses"
- A combination of reports and popular blog articles
- A printable quote (for photographers, artists, and graphic designers)
- A desktop wallpaper, such as the monthly free designs on goinghometoroost.com
- A free tutorial or pattern
- A style guide
- An extremely useful newsletter, similar to the industry updates offered by Abby Glassenberg or Amy Lynn Andrews

#3 Be Consistent in Your Efforts

When you stop checking views and start taking consistent action, your business will consistently attract new customers in kind.

FIND NEW CUSTOMERS FOR YOUR BUSINESS

At this time, we know these things for sure:

- You have products or content for sale,
- You've set up an online storefront and/or website (point of sale),
- You're working your social media profiles, and
- It's feeling *all for naught* because nobody's paying any attention.

Worse, and with all of this added information, you're probably feeling the same as many other entrepreneurs: Who has time to *create* offers and *market* them as well?! I feel you. It's a lot of work to get any small business off the ground, and an online business is no different

First of all, you don't need everyone to find your business, you only need one ideal customer. Then another. Then, you'll aim for a roomful of her, and so on and so forth.

As you're building your business, hone your efforts on finding one perfect customer at a time. At the end of the day, she's the only thing that matters to your bottom line. Therefore, don't post, share, and pin your product onto every wall and feed you can access. Do start having conversations with the right people in the right places.

Here are three simple ways to successfully reach and connect with ideal customers.

#1 Create an Offer

I've said it before, and it bears repeating. These days, nobody just gets traffic. You have to earn it. That means giving your visitors a reason to click or a visual experience that they can't resist. And let's be clear here: you really have to work to create this experience for every visitor you want to greet.

I can't stress the importance of the offer enough. Listing your business online will not grant you traffic, sales, or subscribers. You have to do the marketing legwork and reach out to the visitors you seek.

#2 Social Media Referrals

Online business is a rapidly evolving industry. There is always a new platform on the horizon, and in most cases, my traffic increases by about

400% when I learn how to utilize the platform of the moment. This used to be Facebook, then it was Pinterest, now it's Instagram. Tomorrow it could be Facebook again, or something new altogether. When I get the workings of a social platform down, it refers hundreds, sometimes thousands of visitors to my website every day.

If you're not getting a lot of traffic referrals from social media—it's one of two things:

1. Your images aren't appealing, or
2. The content doesn't serve others.

Pinterest and Instagram have taught me a ton about visuals. While readers have always been skimmers (in other words, content does better with headlines and bullets that the reader can skim), people these days are bombarded with messages everywhere they look, and attention spans are shorter than ever before.

Therefore, skimmers have become scanners—meaning, they're scanning the story or product page for something they can use to make quick visual sense of what they're seeing.

How do you learn what works on visual platforms? Pay attention to what's already getting thousands of repins and "likes." Look for your market's most popular social media leaders and self-critique your efforts against theirs.

Social media is a great marketing tool, but posts on most platforms have a terribly short life-span. Twitter posts are gone within seconds, most Instagram posts are buried within a few hours, and you're lucky if anybody sees your Facebook posts at all!

My favorite platforms offer compound interest on your time invested. For example, on Pinterest your post actually becomes more popular over time. If you use hashtags correctly on Instagram, you can create the same results with a long-time spot in their "popular posts" category.

#3 Join a Support Group

Fortunately, there are ways to hack social proof. Today we have Pinterest group boards, Facebook groups, membership programs, and clubs to help boost each other's marketing efforts, and it can be extremely effective when done right.

For example, I manage a free-to-join Facebook group titled, Creative Entrepreneurs by *Marketing Creativity*. It focuses solely on cross-promotion, and I've seen as much as a 1,700% increase in post reach because of the group.

However, if you find a highly effective group to join, such as the one I manage, and you're not getting much support … it's not them, it's you.

Again, it's going to be one of two things: Your images aren't appealing, or the content doesn't serve others. These two items have to be perfected in order to find new customers for your website, so if you're doing all of the above and seeing no results, it's time to revisit branding, photography, and your offer (serve people, and serve them well).